THE LIFE OF THE PROPHET
MUHAMMAD
صلى الله عليه وسلم

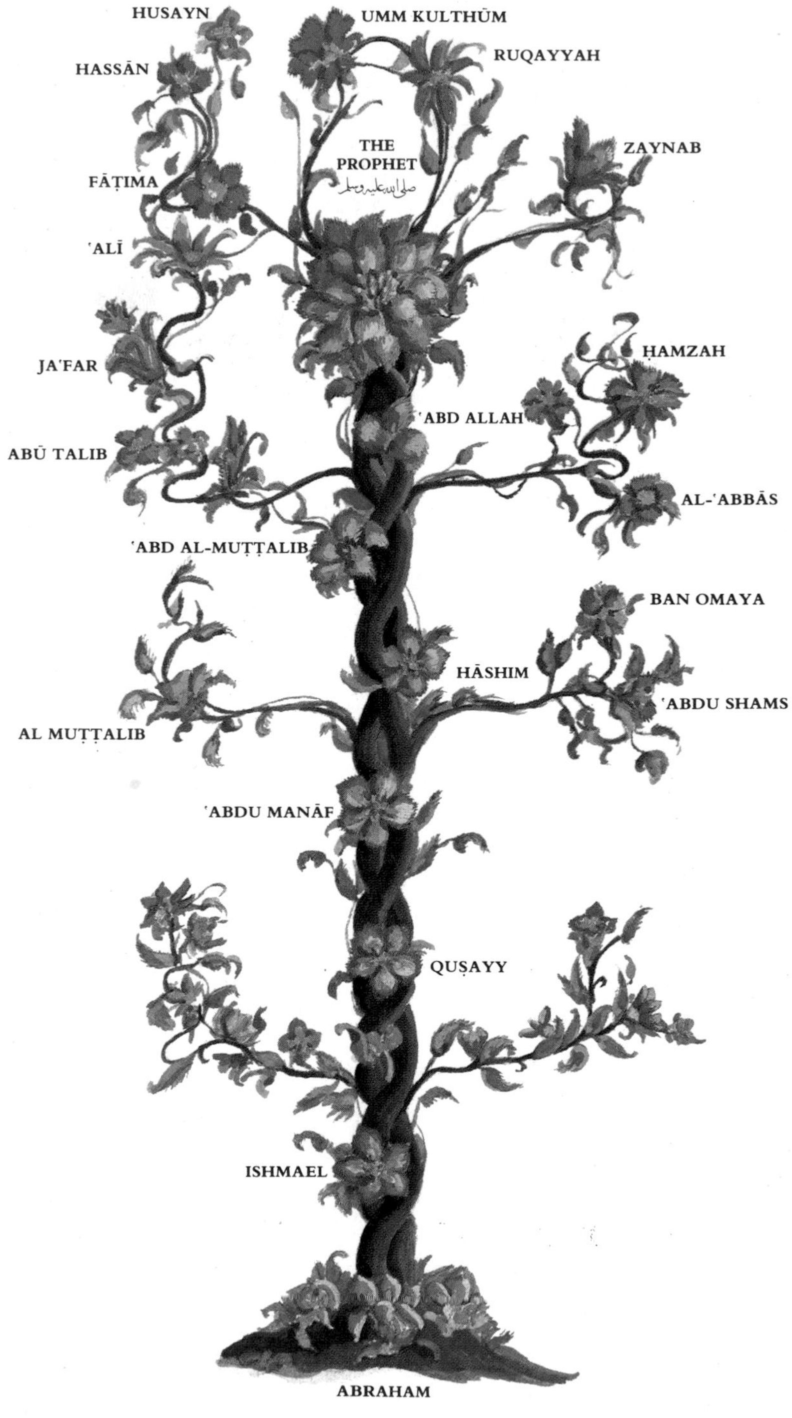

THE PROPHET'S صلى الله عليه وسلم FAMILY TREE

THE LIFE OF THE PROPHET

MUHAMMAD

صلى الله عليه وسلم

by

Leila Azzam

and

Aisha Gouverneur

Illustrations by Mary Hampson Minifie

THE ISLAMIC TEXTS SOCIETY

ACKNOWLEDGEMENTS

The *Sirat Rasul Allah* by Ibn Ishaq (A.H. 85–151) was one of the most useful sources for this children's edition. We wish to acknowledge and thank Dr. Martin Lings, whose manuscript for his *MUHAMMAD his life based on the earliest sources* and advice have been indispensable. Any faults, however, are our own. We would also like to thank Mrs Mary Hampson Minifie for her meticulous and conscientious work in preparing the illustrations for this book.

AUTHORS' NOTE

The use of the traditional salutation after mention of the Prophet in the form of a seal ﷺ has been used throughout the book. It means 'May the Peace and Blessings of Allah be upon him'.

The illustrations do not pretend to depict Muslims from the time of the Prophet ﷺ and his Companions. They have been inspired by images common to much of the Muslim world today.

LA
AG

Published by

The Islamic Texts Society
66 Lincoln's Inn Fields
London WC2A 3LH

Trade orders and all other enquiries should be addressed to:

The Islamic Texts Society
7 Cavendish Avenue
Cambridge CB1 4UP

The Islamic Texts Society is an educational charity, registered in the United Kingdom in 1981. Its aim is to promote a greater understanding of Islam through the publication of English translations of works of traditional importance to the Islamic faith and culture. The Society also publishes editions of hitherto unpublished manuscripts and sponsors original work on Islam by Islamic scholars from all parts of the world.

ISBN 0 946621 01 2 hardback
ISBN 0 946621 02 0 paperback

Designed by The Islamic Texts Society, Cambridge
Production services by Book Production Consultants,
47 Norfolk Street, Cambridge

Set in filmset Bembo 13/15 pt by Oxford University Press, Great Britain.
Printed in Great Britain by Baker Brothers (Litho) Ltd.
and bound by Crawford Brothers (N/C) Ltd.

CONTENTS

LIST OF ILLUSTRATIONS

PREFACE

In the name of Allah the Merciful, the Compassionate. Praise belongs to Allah the Lord of All Being, the Sovereign of the Day of Judgement. There is no God but He and as Allah has blessed Abraham and his family may He bless the Prophet Muhammad ﷺ and his family. Allah is the Glorious and His are all the Praises.

The Islamic Texts Society is pleased to begin its series of children's books with this biography of the Prophet ﷺ, just as it initiated its main work of publishing Islamic texts with the publication of *Muhammad: his life based on the earliest sources* by Dr Martin Lings. In a world for which religion has become increasingly unimportant, the Islamic Texts Society feels that it is essential that children have access to accurate and beautiful books on the fundamentals of Islam. It is a fact to be regretted that so few competently produced religious books exist in a market abundant in attractive books of only worldly consequence. There is no doubt that these books are on the whole conscientious works which provide children with the necessary educational and cultural background, but the increasingly minor role played by religion in modern life is sadly reflected in the relatively unimportant role assigned to books on religion for children. Through its children's series the Islamic Texts Society hopes to place religion at the centre of the child's life rather than at its periphery.

THE ISLAMIC TEXTS SOCIETY
CAMBRIDGE 1985

بسم الله الرحمن الرحيم

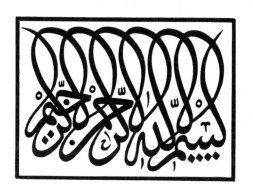

HOW IT ALL BEGAN

NEARLY four thousand years ago, in the Sumerian town of Ur in the valley of the river Euphrates, lived a young man named Abraham. The people of Ur had once worshipped Allah but as time passed they forgot the true religion and started praying to idols, statues made of wood or clay and sometimes even of precious stones.

Even as a small child Abraham could not understand how his people, and especially his father, could make these images with their own hands, call them gods, and then worship them. He had always refused to join his people when they paid respect to these statues. Instead he would leave the town and sit alone, thinking about the heavens and the world about him. He was sure his people were doing wrong and so alone he searched for the right way.

One clear night as he sat staring at the sky he saw a beautiful shining star, so beautiful that he cried out: 'This must be Allah!' He looked at it in awe for some time, until suddenly it began to fade and then it disappeared. He turned away in disappointment saying:

I love not things that set.

(*Koran* vi.77)

On another night Abraham was again looking at the sky and he saw the rising moon, so big and bright that he felt he could almost touch it. He thought to himself:

This is my Lord.

(*Koran* vi.78)

But it was not long before the moon set as well. Then he said,

Unless my Lord guide me, I surely
shall become one of the folk who are astray.

(*Koran* vi.78)

Abraham then saw the beauty and splendour of the sunrise and decided that the sun must be the biggest and most powerful thing in the universe. But for the third time he was wrong, for the sun set at the end of the day. It was then that he realised that Allah is the Most Powerful, the Creator of the stars, the moon, the sun, the earth and of all living things. Suddenly he felt himself totally at peace, because he knew that he had found the Truth.

When he said unto his father and his folk:
What do you worship?
They said: We worship idols, and are ever devoted to them.
He said: Do they hear you when you cry?
Or do they benefit or harm you?
They said: Nay, but we found our fathers
acting in this manner.

He said: See now that which you worship,
You and your forefathers!
Lo! they are (all) an enemy to me, except
the Lord of the Worlds.
Who created me, and He guides me,
And Who feeds me and waters me.
And when I sicken, then He heals me.
And Who causes me to die,
then gives me life (again)
And Who, I ardently hope, will forgive me
my sin on the Day of Judgement.

(*Koran* xxvi.70–82)

One day, while all the townspeople were out, Abraham angrily smashed all the idols with his right hand except for one which was very large. When the people returned they were furious. They remembered the things Abraham had said about the idols. They had him brought forth before everyone and demanded, *'Is it you who did this to our gods, O Abraham?'* Abraham replied, *But this their chief did it. Ask them, if they are able to speak.'* The people exclaimed, *'You know they do not speak.' 'Do you worship what you yourselves have carved when Allah created you and what you make?'* Abraham continued, *'Do you worship instead of Allah that which cannot profit you at all, nor harm you?'*

(*Koran* xxxvii.95–6)
(*Koran* xxi.66)

Finally, Abraham warned them,

Serve Allah, and keep your duty unto Him; that
is better for you if you did but know.
You serve instead of Allah only idols, and you
only invent a lie. Lo! those whom you serve instead
of Allah own no provision for you. So seek your
provision from Allah, and serve Him, and give thanks
unto Him, (for) unto Him you will be brought back.

(*Koran* xxix.16–17)

The people of Ur decided to give Abraham the worst punishment they could find: he was to be burnt to death. On the chosen day all the people

gathered in the centre of the city and even the King of Ur was there. Abraham was then placed inside a special building filled with wood. The wood was lit. Soon the fire became so strong that the people were pushed back by the flames. But Allah said:

O fire, be coolness and peace for Abraham.

(*Koran* xxi.69)

The people waited until the fire had completely died down, and it was then that they saw Abraham still sitting there as though nothing had happened! At that moment they were utterly confused. They were not, however, moved by the miracle that had just happened before their very eyes. Still Abraham tried to persuade his own dear father, who was named Azar, not to worship powerless, un-seeing, un-hearing statues. Abraham explained that special knowledge had come to him and implored his father, '*So follow me and I will lead you on the right path. O my father! Don't serve the Devil.*' But Azar would not listen. He threatened his son with stoning if he continued to reject the gods of Ur. He ordered Abraham to leave the city with these words: '*Depart from me a long while.*' Abraham said, '*Peace be upon you! I shall ask my Lord's forgiveness for you. Surely He was ever gracious to me.*'

(*Koran* xix.43–7)

Imagine how terrible it must have been for him to leave his home, his family and all that he knew, and set out across the wilderness into the unknown. But at the same time, how could he have remained among people who did not believe in Allah and who worshipped statues? Abraham always had a sense that Allah cared for him and he felt Allah near him as he travelled.

At last, after a long hard journey, he arrived at a place by the Mediterranean Sea, not far from Egypt. There he married a noble woman by the name of Sarah and settled in the land of Palestine.

Many years passed but Abraham and his wife were not blessed with any children. In the hope that there would be a child, and in keeping with tradition, Sarah suggested that Abraham should marry Hagar, her Egyptian handmaid. Soon after this took place, Hagar had a little boy named Ishmael.

Some time later Allah promised Abraham another son, but this time the mother of the child would be his first wife, Sarah. This second son would be

called Isaac. Allah also told Abraham that from his two sons—Ishmael and Isaac—two nations and three religions would be founded and because of this he must take Hagar and Ishmael away from Palestine to a new land. These events were an important part of Allah's plan, for the descendants of Ishmael would form a nation from which would come a great Prophet, who would guide the people in the way of Allah. This was to be Muḥammad, the Messenger of Allah, ﷺ. From the descendants of Sarah's child, Isaac, would come Moses and Jesus.

So it was that Abraham, Hagar, and Ishmael left Palestine. They travelled for many days until finally they reached the arid valley of Bacca (later to be called Mecca), which was on one of the great caravan routes. There was no water in the valley and although Hagar and Ishmael only had a small supply of water left, Abraham left them there knowing Allah would take care of them.

Soon all the water was gone. The child began to grow weak from thirst. There were two hills nearby, one called Safā and the other Marwah. Hagar went up one hill and looked into the distance to see if she could find any water, but found none. So she went to the other hill and did the same. She did this seven times. Then sadly she returned to her son, and to her great surprise and joy she found a spring of water bubbling out of the earth near him. This spring, near which the mother and child settled, was later called Zamzam. The area around it became a place of rest for the caravans travelling across the desert and in time grew into the famous trading city of Mecca.

From time to time Abraham travelled from Palestine to visit his family and he saw Ishmael grow into a strong young man. It was during one of these visits that Allah commanded them to rebuild the Ka'bah—the very first place where people had worshipped Allah.

They were told exactly where and how to build it. It was to be erected by the well of Zamzam and built in the shape of a cube. In its eastern corner was to be placed a black stone that had fallen to earth from heaven. An angel brought the stone to them from the nearby hill of Abū Qubays.

Abraham and Ishmael worked hard to rebuild the Ka'bah and as they did so they prayed to Allah to send a Prophet from among their descendants.

And when Abraham and Ishmael were raising
the foundations of the House, (Abraham prayed):
'Our Lord! Receive this from us;
Thou, only Thou, art the All-hearing, the All-knowing;

Our Lord! And make us submissive unto
Thee and of our seed a nation submissive unto
Thee, and show us our ways of worship, and turn
toward us. Lo! Thou, only Thou, art the
Relenting, the Merciful.

Our Lord! And raise up in their midst
a messenger from among them who shall recite unto
them Thy revelations, and shall instruct them in
the Scripture and in wisdom and shall make them
grow. Lo! Thou, only Thou, art the Mighty, Wise.

(*Koran* ii.127–9)

When the Ka'bah was completed, Allah commanded Abraham to call mankind to pilgrimage to His Holy House. Abraham wondered how anyone could hear his call. Allah said, 'You call and I will bring them.' This was how the pilgrimage to the Ka'bah in Mecca was established and when Muslims make the pilgrimage today they continue to answer the age-old call of Abraham.

THE CHILDREN OF ISHMAEL

OVER the years Ishmael's children themselves had children. His descendants increased and formed tribes which spread out all over Arabia. One of these tribes was called Quraysh. Its people never moved away from Mecca and always lived near the Ka'bah.

One of the duties of the leader of Quraysh was to look after those who came on pilgrimage to the Ka'bah. The pilgrims would come from all over Arabia and it was a great honour to provide them with food and water.

As time passed, however, the Arabs stopped worshipping Allah directly and started bringing idols back with them from the different countries they visited. These idols were placed at the Ka'bah, which was no longer regarded as the Sanctuary of Allah, as Abraham had intended it. It was, however, still respected by the Arabs. Around this time the well of Zamzam disappeared beneath the sand.

Also at this time, Quṣayy, one of the leaders of Quraysh, became ruler over Mecca. He held the keys of the temple and had the right to give water to the pilgrims, to feed them, to take charge of meetings, and to hand out war banners before battle. It was also in his house that Quraysh settled their affairs.

After Quṣayy's death, his son 'Abdu Manāf, who had become famous during his father's lifetime, took over the leadership of Quraysh. After him came his son Hāshim. It is said that Hāshim was the first to begin the two great caravan journeys of Quraysh, one in the summer to Syria and the north, and one in the winter to Yemen and the south. As a result, Mecca grew rich and became a large and important centre of trade.

One summer Hāshim went north to buy goods to sell in Yemen. On his way he stopped in Yathrib to trade in the market and there he saw a beautiful woman. She was Salmà, the daughter of 'Amr ibn Zeid, who was from a much respected family. Hāshim proposed marriage to her and was accepted because he was an honourable and distinguished man. In time, Salmà gave birth to a beautiful son and as some of his hair was white they called him Shaybah, which in Arabic means 'grey-haired'. Mother and son stayed in the cooler, healthier climate of Yathrib, while Hāshim returned to Mecca, but he would visit them each time he took his caravan to the north. During one of these journeys, however, Hāshim became ill and died.

Shaybah, a handsome, intelligent boy, grew up in his uncle's house in Yathrib. He was proud of being the son of Ḥāshim ibn 'Abdi Manāf, the head of Quraysh, guardian of the Ka'bah and protector of the pilgrims, even though he had not known his father, who had died while Shaybah was very young.

At Hāshim's death his brother al-Muṭṭalib took over his duties and responsibilities. He travelled to Yathrib to see his nephew, Shaybah, and decided that as the boy would one day inherit his father's place, the time had come for him to live in Mecca.

It was hard for Salmà, Shaybah's mother, to let her son go with his uncle but she finally realized that it was for the best. Al-Muṭṭalib returned to Mecca, entering the city at noon on his camel with Shaybah behind him. When the people of Mecca saw the boy they thought he was a slave and, pointing at him, called out ‘ʿAbd al-Muṭṭalib’, ‘ʿAbd’ being the Arabic for ‘slave’. Al-Muṭṭalib told them that Shaybah was not a slave but his nephew who had come to live with them. From that day on, however, Shaybah was always affectionately called ʿAbd al-Muṭṭalib.

On the death of al-Muṭṭalib, who died in Yemen where he had gone to trade, ʿAbd al-Muṭṭalib took his place. He became the most respected member of his family, loved and admired by all. He was, however, unlike those Arabs who had given up the teachings of Abraham.

THE PROMISE AT ZAMZAM

THE well of Zamzam, which disappeared when the Arabs placed idols at the Ka'bah, remained buried under the sand. Thus, for many years the people of Quraysh had to fetch their water from far away. One day 'Abd al-Muṭṭalib was very tired from doing this and fell asleep next to the Ka'bah. He had a dream in which he was told to dig up Zamzam. When he woke up he was puzzled because he did not know what Zamzam was, the well having disappeared many years before he was born. The next day he had the same dream, but this time he was told where to find the well.

'Abd al-Muṭṭalib had one son at that time, and together they began to dig. The work was so difficult that 'Abd al-Muṭṭalib made an oath to Allah that if one day he were to have ten sons to help him and stand by him, in return he would sacrifice one of them in Allah's honour. After working for three days they finally found the well of Zamzam. Pilgrims have been drinking from it ever since.

The years passed by and 'Abd al-Muṭṭalib did have ten sons. They grew into fine, strong men and the time came for him to keep his promise to Allah. He told his sons about the promise and they agreed that he had to sacrifice one of them. To see which one it would be, they decided to draw lots, which was the custom of Quraysh when deciding important matters. 'Abd al-Muṭṭalib told each son to get an arrow and write his own name upon it and then to bring it to him. This they did, after which he took them to the Ka'bah where there was a man whose special task it was to cast arrows and pick one from among them. This man solemnly proceeded to do this. On the arrow he chose was written the name of 'Abd Allāh, the youngest and favourite son of 'Abd al-Muṭṭalib. Even so, the father took his son near the Ka'bah and prepared to sacrifice him.

Many of the Quraysh leaders were present and they became very angry because 'Abd Allāh was very young and much loved by everyone. They tried to think of a way to save his life. Someone suggested that the advice of a wise old woman who lived in Yathrib should be sought, and so 'Abd al-Muṭṭalib took his son and went to see if she could decide what to do. Some of the Meccans went with them and when they got there the woman asked, 'What is the price of a man's life?'

They told her, 'Ten camels', for at that time if one man killed another, his family would have to give ten camels to the dead man's family in order to keep the peace among them. So the woman told them to go back to the Ka'bah and draw lots between 'Abd Allāh and ten camels. If the camels were chosen, they were to be killed and the meat given to the poor. If 'Abd Allāh was picked then ten more camels were to be added and the lots drawn again and again until they finally fell on the camels.

'Abd al-Muṭṭalib returned to the Ka'bah with his son and the people of Mecca. There they started to draw lots between 'Abd Allāh and the camels, starting with ten camels. 'Abd al-Muṭṭalib prayed to Allah to spare his son and everyone waited in silence for the result. The choice fell on 'Abd Allāh, so his father added ten more camels. Again the choice fell on 'Abd Allah, so they did the same thing again and again, adding ten camels each time. Finally they reached one hundred camels, and only then did the lot fall on the camels.

'Abd Allāh was saved and everyone was very happy. 'Abd al-Muṭṭalib, however, wanted to make sure that this was the true result so he repeated the draw three times and each time it fell on the camels. He then gave thanks to Allah that He had spared 'Abd Allāh's life. The camels were sacrificed and there was enough food for the entire city, even the animals and birds.

'Abd Allāh grew up to be a handsome young man and his father eventually chose Āminah, the daughter of Wahb, as a wife for him. It was a good match, for she was the finest of Quraysh women and 'Abd Allāh the best of the men. He spent several months with his wife but then he had to leave her and travel with one of the caravans to trade with Syria. On his way back to Mecca from Syria 'Abd Allāh became ill and had to stop off in Yathrib to recover. The caravan, however, continued on its way and arrived back in Mecca without him. On hearing of 'Abd Allāh's illness, 'Abd al-Muṭṭalib sent another son, al-Ḥārith, to bring 'Abd Allāh back to Mecca, but he was too late. When he arrived in Yathrib 'Abd Allāh was dead.

Āminah was heart-broken to lose her husband and the father of the child she would soon give birth to. Only Allah knew that this orphan child would one day be a great Prophet.

THE ELEPHANT REFUSES TO MOVE

ABRAHAH, who came from Abyssinia—a country in Africa—conquered Yemen and was made vice-regent there. Later, he noticed that at a certain time of the year large numbers of people would travel from all over Yemen and the rest of Arabia to Mecca. He asked the reason for this and was told that they were going on pilgrimage to the Ka'bah.

Abrahah hated the idea of Mecca being more important than his own country, so he decided to build a church of coloured marble, with doors of gold and ornaments of silver, and ordered the people to visit it instead of the Ka'bah. But no one obeyed him.

Abrahah became angry and decided to destroy the Ka'bah. He prepared a large army led by an elephant and set off towards Mecca. When the Meccans heard that he was coming they became very frightened. Abrahah's army was huge and they could not fight it. But how could they let him destroy the Holy Ka'bah? They went to ask the advice of their leader, 'Abd al-Muṭṭalib.

When Abrahah arrived outside Mecca, 'Abd al-Muṭṭalib went to meet him. Abrahah said, 'What do you want?'

Abrahah had taken 'Abd al-Muṭṭalib's camels, which he had found grazing as he entered Mecca, so 'Abd al-Muṭṭalib replied, 'I want my camels back.'

Abrahah was very surprised and said, 'I have come to destroy your Holy Ka'bah, the holy place of your fathers, and you ask me about some camels?'

'Abd al-Muṭṭalib replied calmly, 'The camels belong to me; the Ka'bah belongs to Allah and He will protect it.' Then he left Abrahah and went back to Quraysh and ordered them to leave Mecca and wait for their enemies in the mountains.

In the morning Abrahah prepared to enter the town. He put armour on his elephant and drew up his troops for battle. He intended to destroy the Ka'bah and then return to Yemen. At that moment, however, the elephant knelt down and refused to get up, no matter how much the soldiers tried to get it to move by beating it. But when they turned its face in the direction of Yemen it immediately got up and started off. In fact, it did the same in any other direction, but as soon as they pointed it towards Mecca it knelt down again.

Suddenly, flocks of birds appeared from over the sea. Each bird carried three stones as small as peas and they dropped them on Abrahah's army. The soldiers suddenly fell ill. Even Abrahah was hit by the stones and fled in fear with the rest of his army back to Yemen, where he later died. On seeing their enemy flee the Arabs came down from the mountains to the Ka'bah and gave thanks to Allah.

After this, Quraysh gained great respect and became known as 'the people of Allah', and the year in which these events took place, 570 A.D., was named the 'Year of the Elephant'. In that year Allah had saved the Ka'bah and he would soon bring forth a Prophet from among Quraysh.

In the Name of Allah, the Beneficent, the Merciful

Hast thou not seen how thy Lord dealt with the owners of the Elephant?
Did He not bring their stratagem to naught,
And send against them swarms of flying creatures,
Which pelted them with stones of baked clay,
And made them like green crops devoured (by cattle)?

(*Koran* cv.1–5)

THE PROPHET IS BORN

ONE day, while travelling north, one of the Arab tribes from Mecca met a hermit in the desert. Some of the men stopped to speak with him. Hermits were known to be wise and the Arabs often asked their advice.

The hermit asked where they had come from. When they replied that they were from Mecca, he told them that Allah would soon send a prophet, who

would come from their people. They asked the name of this prophet and the hermit answered that his name would be Muḥammad and that he would guide them to a new way of life.

Meanwhile in Mecca, Āminah, although saddened by the loss of her husband, felt especially well and strong as she awaited the birth of her baby. During this time she dreamt of many things. On one occasion it was as if a great light were shining out of her, and on another she heard a voice telling her that she would have a boy and that his name would be Muḥammad. She never forgot that voice but she told no one about it.

On Monday, the twelfth day of Rabi al-Awwal in the Year of the Elephant, Āminah gave birth to a son. Allah sends man many signs when one of His chosen Prophets is born. And on that twelfth day of Rabi al-Awwal in the year 570 A.D., many such signs were seen. Some were seen by Jewish scholars who had read in their scriptures of a coming Prophet. One of these learned men in Yathrib, for instance, saw a brilliant new star he had never seen before as he studied the heavens that night. He called the people around him and, pointing the star out to them, told them a Prophet must have been born.

That same night another Jew was passing by the meeting place of the leaders of Quraysh in Mecca. He asked them if a baby boy had just been born and told them that if it were true, this would be the Prophet of the Arab nation.

Āminah sent news of the birth to her father-in-law, 'Abd al-Muṭṭalib, who was sitting near the Ka'bah at the time. He was very happy and began at once to think of a name for the boy. An ordinary name would not do. Six days came and went and still he had not decided. But on the seventh day, as he lay asleep near the Ka'bah, 'Abd al-Muṭṭalib dreamt that he should give the baby the unusual name of Muḥammad, just as Āminah herself had dreamt. And so the child was called Muḥammad ﷺ, which means 'the Praised One'.

When 'Abd al-Muṭṭalib told the leaders of Quraysh what he had named his grandson, many of them asked, 'Why did you not choose the sort of name that is used by our people?'

At once he replied, 'I want him to be praised by Allah in the heavens and praised by men on earth.'

A TIME WITH ḤALĪMAH

Like many other women in Mecca, Āminah decided to send her son away from the city for his early years to the desert where it was more healthy. Women from the desert used to come to Mecca to collect the new babies and they would then keep them until they developed into strong children, for which they were well paid by the parents.

Among the women who travelled to Mecca to fetch a new baby at the time Āminah's son was born, was a Bedouin woman called Ḥalīmah. With her was her husband and baby son. They had always been very poor, but this year things were harder than ever because there had been famine. The donkey that carried Ḥalīmah on the journey was so weak from hunger that he often stumbled. Ḥalīmah's own baby son cried all the time because his mother could not feed him properly. Even their she-camel did not give them one drop of milk. Ḥalīmah did not know what to do. She thought to herself, 'How can I possibly feed another baby when I haven't got enough milk even for my own son?'

At last they reached Mecca. All the other women of the tribe to which Ḥalīmah belonged, the Bani Sa'd, found a child to take back with them, but not Ḥalīmah. The only baby left was Muḥammad ﷺ. Usually the father paid the wet-nurse but Muḥammad's father was dead. So no one wanted to take him, even though he was from one of the noblest families of Quraysh. Ḥalīmah did not want to take him either, but she did not want to be the only woman to go back to her tribe without a baby to bring up. She asked her husband whether she should take Muḥammad ﷺ or not. He advised her to do so, adding, 'Perhaps Allah will bless us because of him.'

They started on the return journey and as soon as Ḥalīmah began to feed Muḥammad ﷺ her milk suddenly increased and she had enough for him as

well as her baby son. When they were back home, everything began to change. The land became green, and the date trees, one of their main sources of food, gave lots of fruit. Even the sheep and their old she-camel began to give plenty of milk. Ḥalīmah and her husband knew that this good fortune had come because they had the new baby, Muḥammad ﷺ, whom they had come to love as if he were their own son.

When Muḥammad ﷺ was two years old, Ḥalīmah took him back to his mother. She pleaded with Āminah, however, to let her keep him for a little longer, and to her great joy the mother agreed.

During his time with Ḥalīmah's family in the desert, Muḥammad ﷺ played with her children and together they would take the sheep out to graze. At other times, however, Ḥalīmah would often find him sitting alone.

It is said that on one occasion, two angels came to Muḥammad ﷺ and washed his heart with snow. In this way Allah made his heart pure for He intended Muḥammad ﷺ to be greater than any man ever born and to become the Seal of the Prophets.

In the Name of Allah, the Beneficent, the Merciful

Did We not expand thy breast for thee
And eased thee of thy burden
Which weighed down thy back;
And exalted thy fame?
So truly with hardship comes ease,
Truly with hardship comes ease.
So when thou art relieved, still toil
And strive to please thy Lord.

(*Koran* xciv.1–8)

When Ḥalīmah finally took Muḥammad ﷺ back to Āminah, he was a healthy, strong boy. Later he would look back with joy on the time he had spent with Ḥalīmah, and he always thought of himself as one of the Bani Sa'd.

THE ORPHAN'S CHILDHOOD

MUḤAMMAD ﷺ returned to live with his mother in Mecca when he was about three years old. Three years later Āminah decided to take her son to visit his uncles in Yathrib. She told her maid, Barakah, to prepare everything they would need for the long journey, and then they joined one of the caravans going there.

They stayed in Yathrib a month and Muḥammad ﷺ enjoyed the visit with his cousins. The climate there was very pleasant and he learned to swim and to fly a kite. On their way back to Mecca, however, Āminah became ill and died. She was buried in the village at al-Abwa not far from Yathrib. Muḥammad ﷺ returned sadly to Mecca with his mother's maid. He was now six years old and had lost both his father and mother. He was then adopted by his grandfather, ʿAbd al-Muṭṭalib, who loved him dearly and kept him by his side at all times.

It was the custom of ʿAbd al-Muṭṭalib to sit on a blanket near the Kaʿbah. There he was always surrounded by people who had come to speak to him. No one was allowed to sit on the blanket with him, however, except his grandson Muḥammad ﷺ, which shows how close they were to each other. Many times ʿAbd al-Muṭṭalib was heard to say: 'This boy will be very important one day.'

Two years later ʿAbd al-Muṭṭalib became ill and Muḥammad ﷺ stayed by him constantly. ʿAbd al-Muṭṭalib told his son, Abū Ṭālib, to adopt Muḥammad ﷺ after his death, which he did. Abū Ṭālib had many children of his own, but Muḥammad ﷺ immediately became part of his family and the favourite child.

The time came for Quraysh to prepare a caravan to go to Syria. Abū Ṭālib was going with them and he took Muḥammad ﷺ along. It was Muḥammad's first journey to the north. After days of travel, the caravan arrived at a place near Syria where the Romans used to come to trade with the Arabs. Near this marketplace lived a monk called Baḥīrà. His cell had been used by generations of monks before him and contained ancient manuscripts.

Baḥīrà saw the caravan in the distance and was amazed to see that over it was a large white cloud. It was the only cloud in a clear blue sky and it appeared to be shading one of the travellers. The monk was even more surprised to see that the cloud seemed to follow the caravan but disappeared when the person it was shading sat down under a tree. Baḥīrà knew from the scriptures that a prophet was expected to come after Jesus and it had been his wish to see this prophet before he died. Realizing that what he had just seen was a miracle, he began to think that his wish might, after all, come true.

The monk sent an invitation to the Meccans to come and eat with him. The Arabs were surprised because they often passed by and Baḥīrà had never invited them before. When the group was all together for the meal, the monk said, 'Is this everyone?'

'No', someone said, 'a boy was left watching the camels.'

Baḥīrà insisted that the boy should join them. The boy was Muḥammad ﷺ. When he arrived Baḥīra said nothing, but watched him all through the meal. He noticed many things about his appearance which fitted the description in the old manuscripts. Later on he took him aside and asked Muḥammad ﷺ many questions. He soon found out how he felt about the idols in the Ka'bah. When Baḥīrà tried to make him swear by them, as the Arabs used to do, Muḥammad ﷺ said, 'There is nothing in this world that I hate more'. They talked together about Allah, and about Muḥammad's life and family. What was said made Baḥīrà certain that this was indeed the Prophet who would follow Jesus.

Then the monk went to Abū Ṭālib and asked him how he was related to Muḥammad ﷺ. Abū Ṭālib told him that Muḥammad ﷺ was his son. Baḥīrà replied that this could not be so because thc boy was destined to grow up an orphan, and he ordered Abū Ṭālib to watch over Muḥammad ﷺ with great care.

There are many stories told about Muḥammad's youth. Some tell of how he used to take the family's sheep to graze and was always kind to them. While they grazed he would sit thinking about the mysteries of nature. Unlike those around him, he never worshipped the idols and never swore by them. He also wondered why people were always struggling for power and money, and this saddened him and made him feel lonely, but he kept his feelings to himself. He was a quiet, thoughtful boy, and rarely played with other boys of his age.

On one occasion, however, Muḥammad ﷺ went with some of the boys to a wedding in Mecca. When he reached the house he heard the sounds of music and dancing but just as he was about to enter he suddenly felt tired and, sitting down, fell asleep. He didn't wake up until late the next morning and thus missed the celebrations. In this way Allah prevented him from doing anything foolish for He was keeping Muḥammad ﷺ for something much more important.

THE PROPHET'S MARRIAGE

By the time Muḥammad ﷺ was twenty-five he was famous for his honesty. He was respected by everyone, even the elders of Mecca. The purity of his nature increased with the years. It seemed he had an inner knowledge that other people did not have. He believed in one God—Creator of the world—and he worshipped Him with all his heart and with all his soul. Muḥammad ﷺ was the finest of his people, the most kind, truthful and reliable person in Mecca. He was known among Quraysh as 'the trustworthy' (al-Amīn) because of the good qualities Allah had given him. He spent many quiet hours in a cave in Mount Ḥirā', not far from Mecca, thinking about Allah.

Among Quraysh was a respected and wealthy woman named Khadījah. She was involved in trade and on hearing of Muḥammad's reputation, sent for him and asked him to take her goods and trade with them in Syria. Muḥammad ﷺ agreed and left for Syria with one of Khadījah's caravans. With him went her slave, Maysarah, and they spent a great deal of time talking together. Maysarah soon came to admire Muḥammad ﷺ. He thought he was quite different from all the other men of Quraysh.

Two unusual events took place during this journey which puzzled Maysarah very much. The first happened when they stopped to rest near the lonely home of a monk. Muḥammad ﷺ sat under a tree while Maysarah was busy with some work. The monk came up to Maysarah and asked, 'Who is the man resting under the tree?'

'One of Quraysh, the people who guard the Ka'bah', said Maysarah.

'No one but a Prophet is sitting beneath this tree', replied the monk.

The second event occurred on the journey back to Mecca. It happened at noon, when the sun is at its hottest. Maysarah was riding behind Muḥammad

ﷺ and as the sun grew hotter he saw two angels appear above Muḥammad ﷺ and shield him from the sun's harmful rays.

The trading was very successful and Muḥammad ﷺ made more profit for Khadījah than she had ever received before. When they arrived back in Mecca Maysarah told Khadījah everything about the trip and what he had noticed about Muḥammad's character and behaviour.

Khadījah was a widow in her forties and as well as being rich and highly respected she was also very beautiful. Many men wanted to marry her but none of them suited her. When she met Muḥammad ﷺ, however, she thought he was very special. She sent a friend to ask Muḥammad ﷺ why he was not married. Muḥammad ﷺ said that it was because he had no money, to which the friend replied: 'Supposing a rich, beautiful and noble lady agreed to marry you?' Muḥammad ﷺ wanted to know who that could be. The friend told him it was Khadījah. Muḥammad ﷺ was very happy, because he greatly respected Khadījah. He went with his uncles, Abū Ṭālib and Ḥamzah, to Khadījah's uncle, and asked his permission to marry her. The uncle gave his permission and soon after, Muḥammad ﷺ and Khadījah were married.

Their marriage was a joyful one and Muḥammad ﷺ and Khadījah were well suited. Their life together, however, was not without some sadness. They were blessed with six children, two sons and four daughters. Sadly their first born, a son called Qāsim, died shortly before his second birthday, and their last child, also a son, only lived for a short time. Happily, their four daughters—Zaynab, Ruqayyah, Umm Kulthūm, and Fāṭimah—all survived.

For a few years Muḥammad ﷺ lived a calm and quiet life as a merchant in Mecca. His wisdom benefited many people. One such time was when Quraysh decided to rebuild the Ka'bah. It was a difficult decision for them because they had to knock it down before rebuilding it and the people were afraid that Allah might be angry with them for knocking down His sanctuary. At last one of the wise old men of Quraysh decided to begin, then everybody followed him.

They worked until they reached down to the first foundation that Abraham had built. As soon as they began to remove the stones of this foundation, however, the whole of Mecca began to shake. They were so afraid that they decided to leave these stones where they were and build on top of them.

Each tribe brought stones and they built the Ka'bah up until they reached the place where the black stone was to be set. They then began to argue about who should have the honour of carrying the black stone and lifting it to its place in one of the corners of the Ka'bah. They almost came to blows but fortunately one of the men offered a solution. He suggested that they should be guided by the first person to enter the place of worship. They all agreed and as Muḥammad ﷺ was the first to enter everyone was pleased, because they all trusted him.

They told him the cause of the argument and he asked them to bring a large cloak. They did as he asked, and after spreading the cloak on the ground he placed the black stone in the centre of it. Then he asked a man from each tribe to hold one edge of the cloak and together to raise it to the height where the stone should be set. When this was done, he took the stone off the cloak and put it into place himself.

This story shows how all Quraysh respected and trusted Muḥammad ﷺ and how, by his wisdom and good sense, he was able to keep the peace.

THE COMING OF THE ARCHANGEL GABRIEL

MUḤAMMAD ﷺ believed that there was only one Allah, Creator of the sun, the moon, the earth, the sky, and of all living things, and that all people should worship only Him. Muḥammad ﷺ would often leave the crowded city and go to the cave in Mount Ḥirā'. He liked to be alone there, away from all thoughts of the world and daily life, eating and drinking little.

In his fortieth year, Muḥammad ﷺ left Mecca to spend Ramadan, the traditional month of retreat, in the cave. In the second half of Ramadan, Allah began to reveal His message for mankind through Muḥammad ﷺ. This first Revelation occurred as follows. The Archangel Gabriel came to Muḥammad ﷺ in the cave and commanded him to 'Read'.

Muḥammad ﷺ replied 'I cannot read.'

At this the Archangel took Muḥammad ﷺ in his arms and pressed him to him until it was almost too much to bear. He then released him and said again 'Read.'

'I cannot', replied Muḥammad ﷺ, at which the Archangel embraced him again. For the third time the Archangel commanded Muḥammad ﷺ to read, but still he said he could not and was again embraced. On releasing him this time, however, the Archangel Gabriel said:

Read: In the Name of thy Lord who createth,
Createth man from a clot.
Read: And thy Lord is the Most Generous
Who teacheth by the pen,
Teacheth man that which he knew not.

(*Koran* xcvi.1–5)

Muḥammad ﷺ repeated these verses, just as the Archangel had said them. When the Archangel was sure Muḥammad ﷺ knew them by heart, he went away.

Now that he was alone Muḥammad ﷺ could not understand what had happened to him. He was terribly afraid and rushed out of the cave. Perhaps the cave was haunted? Perhaps the devil had taken a hold of his mind?

But he was stopped by a voice from heaven which said: 'O Muḥammad ﷺ, you are the Messenger of Allah, and I am Gabriel.' He looked up at the sky and wherever he turned he saw the Archangel Gabriel.

In a state of confusion he returned home to Khadījah. When his wife saw him she became very worried as he began to shiver, as though in a fever. He asked her to wrap him in blankets, which she did. After a while he recovered sufficiently to tell her what had happened at Ḥirā'. Khadījah believed all that he told her and with great respect said: 'Be happy, O son of my uncle and be confident. Truly I swear by Allah who has my soul in His hands, that you will be our people's Prophet.' Muḥammad ﷺ, the Messenger of Allah, was eased by her faith in him, but after all that had happened he was exhausted and fell fast asleep.

Khadījah left the Prophet ﷺ sleeping and went to see her cousin, Waraqah ibn Nawfal, to ask him what he thought about all that had happened. Waraqah was a very wise man who had read many books and had become a Christian after studying the Bible. He told Khadījah that Muḥammad ﷺ had been chosen by Allah to be His Messenger. Just as the Archangel Gabriel had come to Moses before and had ordered him to guide his people, so, too, would Muḥammad ﷺ be the Prophet of his people. But Waraqah warned that all the people would not listen to the Prophet and some would mistreat his followers. He must, however, be patient because he had a great message for all the world.

From that day on, the Archangel Gabriel came often to the Prophet ﷺ and the verses he taught him, the message from Allah to man, were later written down, and are known to us as the Holy Koran.

THE FIRST MUSLIMS

AFTER that momentous day in the month of Ramadan, Revelation came again and again to the Prophet ﷺ. He understood now what he had to do and prepared himself for what was to come. Only a strong and brave man, helped by Allah, can be a true prophet because people often refuse to listen to Allah's message.

Khadījah was the first to believe the Prophet ﷺ and accept as true what he brought from Allah. Through her, Allah made things easier for the Prophet ﷺ. Khadījah strengthened him, helped him spread his message, and stood up to the people who were against him.

Then Revelation ceased for a time. The Prophet ﷺ was upset and unhappy, thinking that Allah had left him, or that he might have angered Allah in some way so that Allah no longer thought him worthy of His message. However, the Archangel Gabriel came back to him and brought this *surah*, or chapter, of the Koran:

In the Name of Allah, the Beneficent, the Merciful

By the morning hours
And by the night when it is stillest,
Thy Lord hath neither forsaken thee nor doth He hate thee,
And verily the Last will be better for thee
than the First.
And verily thy Lord will give unto thee so that
thou wilt be content.
Did He not find thee an orphan and protect thee?
Did He not find thee wandering and guide thee?
Did He not find thee destitute and enrich thee?

Therefore the orphan oppress not,
Therefore the beggar drive not away,
And as for thy Lord's blessing, declare it.

(*Koran* xciii.1–11)

The Prophet ﷺ began to speak secretly of Allah's message to those who were close to him and whom he could trust. At that time Mecca was going through hard times. There was very little food to be had. Abū Ṭālib, the Prophet's uncle, who had taken care of him after his grandfather's death, was finding it very difficult to feed his large family. The Prophet ﷺ said that he and another uncle, al-'Abbās, who was a rich man, would each bring up one of Abū Ṭālib's children in order to help him. The Prophet ﷺ took 'Alī and his uncle took Ja'far.

One day, when the Prophet ﷺ was outside the city, the Archangel Gabriel appeared to him. The Archangel kicked the side of a hill and a spring of water began to flow out. He then began to wash himself in the running water to show the Prophet ﷺ the ritual ablution to be made before prayer. Then the Archangel showed him all the positions of Muslim prayer—the various movements and things to be said with each movement. The Prophet ﷺ returned home and taught all these things first to Khadījah and then to his followers. Since then Muslims have continued to purify themselves before prayer by performing the ritual ablution and have followed the same movements and prayers first performed by the Prophet ﷺ.

To begin with, though, only the Prophet ﷺ and his wife knew of these things. Then one day 'Alī entered the room and found the Prophet ﷺ and Khadījah praying. He was puzzled and asked what they were doing. The Prophet ﷺ explained to him that they were praising Allah and giving thanks to Him. That night 'Alī stayed up thinking about all that the Prophet ﷺ had said; he had great admiration and respect for his cousin. Finally he came to a decision and the next day he went to the Prophet ﷺ and told him that he wanted to follow him. Thus Khadījah was the first woman to embrace Islam, the teachings which the Prophet ﷺ brought from Allah, and 'Alī was the first young man. Shortly after they were joined by Zayd ibn Hārithah, a slave, freed and adopted by the Prophet ﷺ.

The Prophet ﷺ began to leave Mecca with ʿAlī in order to pray. One day Abū Ṭālib happened to pass by and when he saw them he stopped and asked them what they were doing. The Prophet ﷺ told him that they were praying and following the same religion as Abraham. He explained that, like Abraham, he had been ordered to guide the people to Allah's truth. Abū Ṭālib looked at his son, ʿAlī, and said: 'Muḥammad ﷺ would never make you do anything that was wrong. Go with him. But I cannot leave the religion I now follow and which was followed by my father.' Then he turned to the Prophet ﷺ, saying, 'Even so, I promise you, Muḥammad ﷺ, that no one will hurt you as long as I am alive.' And with that Abū Ṭālib went on his way.

At about this time the news of Muḥammad ﷺ being the Prophet reached an honest, wise, and respected merchant of Mecca called Abū Bakr. He knew Muḥammad ﷺ well and believed he could never lie, so he went to find out for himself if the story were true. The Prophet ﷺ told him that he had indeed been sent by Allah to teach everyone to worship the one true Allah. On hearing this from the Prophet's own lips Abū Bakr knew it to be the truth and became a believer instantly. Later the Prophet ﷺ was reported to have said that everyone he ever invited to accept Islam showed signs of disbelief and doubt, except Abū Bakr; when he was told of it he did not hold back or hesitate.

Because of his wisdom, honesty, and kindness people had always turned to Abū Bakr for advice. He was, therefore, a man of some influence and through him many people came to Islam. Among these was Saʿd ibn Abī Waqqās, the uncle of Āminah, the Prophet's mother. The night before Abū Bakr came to visit him and tell him about Islam, Saʿd ibn Abī Waqqās dreamt that he was walking in darkness. As he walked he saw the moon and when he looked at it he saw ʿAlī, Abū Bakr, and Zayd, the Prophet's freed slave, beckoning to him to come and join them. When Abū Bakr told him about the Prophet's religion, he understood the meaning of his dream and went at once to the Prophet ﷺ and declared himself a Muslim. He understood that to be a Muslim means to submit oneself to Allah's Will and to serve only Him.

Another person brought to Islam by Abū Bakr was Bilāl. One night Abū Bakr went to the house of Umayyah ibn Khalaf, one of the most important men of Quraysh. Umayyah was out and Abū Bakr found only Umayyah's slave, Bilāl, at home. Abū Bakr talked to the slave about Islam and before he left, Bilāl, too, had become a Muslim.

The number of people following the Prophet ﷺ began to grow. Sometimes they would all go out of the city to the mountains around Mecca to hear him recite the Koran and to be taught by him. This was all done very secretly and only a very few people knew about Islam in those early days.

THE TROUBLES BEGIN

THREE years passed and one day the Archangel Gabriel came to the Prophet ﷺ and ordered him to start preaching openly to everyone. So the Prophet ﷺ told the people of Mecca that he had something very important to tell them. He stood on a hillside in Mecca, called Safā, and they gathered around to hear what he had to say.

He started by asking them if they would believe him were he to say that an army was about to attack them. They answered that indeed they would, because he never lied. He then told them that he was the Messenger of Allah, sent to show them the right way, and to warn them of terrible punishments if they did not follow him in worshipping only Allah and none other. Abū Lahab, one of the Prophet's uncles who was among the listeners, suddenly stood up and said, 'May you perish! Did you call us here just to tell us this?'

At this, Allah sent to the Prophet ﷺ the following *sūrah*:

In the Name of Allah, The Beneficent, The Merciful

The Power of Abū Lahab will perish, and he will perish.
His wealth and gains will not save him.
He shall roast at a flaming fire,
And his wife, the carrier of firewood
Will have upon her neck a rope of palm-fibre.

(*Koran* cxi.1–5)

Then the crowd dispersed and the Prophet ﷺ was left alone.

A few days later the Prophet ﷺ tried again. A feast was prepared in his house for all of his uncles. After the meal he spoke to them and said, 'O sons of 'Abd al-Muṭṭalib! I know of no Arab who has come to his people with a better message than mine. I have brought you the best news for this life and the next. Allah has ordered me to call you to Him. So which of you will help me?'

All the men kept silent. Then 'Alī, his cousin, jumped up and said: 'O Prophet of Allah! I will help you.' Then the men all got up and left, laughing as they went because only one young boy had agreed to help the Prophet ﷺ.

His message ignored by most of the people and his uncles, the Prophet ﷺ continued to meet his friends secretly in a house near the hill of Safā. There they prayed together and he taught them about the religion of Islam.

But even though they kept to themselves, they were sometimes abused by those who would not believe. From one such incident, however, an unexpected conversion to Islam took place. One day, when the Prophet ﷺ was returning home, speaking with his followers, he met Abū Jahl, a leader of Quraysh, who hated the Prophet ﷺ and his teachings. Abū Jahl started to insult him and to speak spitefully of Islam, but the Prophet ﷺ made no reply and went on his way.

Later, Ḥamzah, one of the Prophet's uncles, who was a strong and brave warrior of whom people were quite afraid, heard how his nephew had been insulted. Filled with rage, he ran straight to the Ka'bah where Abū Jahl was sitting among the people and struck him a violent blow in the face with his bow. Ḥamzah then shouted, 'Will you insult him when I follow his religion, and I say what he says? Hit me back if you can!' Some people got up to help Abū Jahl but he stopped them saying, 'Leave Ḥamzah alone, for by Allah, I have insulted his nephew badly.'

From that moment on Ḥamzah followed the teachings of the Prophet ﷺ and with his conversion to Islam Quraysh realised that the Prophet ﷺ had a strong supporter and so for a while they stopped persecuting him.

Soon, however, the leaders of Quraysh became angry again, when they saw that the Prophet ﷺ was going ahead with his teaching. A group of them went to his uncle, Abū Ṭālib, who had promised to protect him. They told him to ask the Prophet ﷺ to stop attacking their gods and their way of life, and in return they would let him do as he wished with his religion.

After a time they saw that there was no change, so they went back to Abū Ṭālib and this time they told him that if he did not stop his nephew, they would fight them both. Abū Ṭālib was very upset by this quarrel among his people, but he could not break his word to his nephew. He sent for the Prophet ﷺ and told him what had happened, saying, 'Spare me and spare yourself; do not put a greater burden on me than I can bear.'

The Prophet ﷺ thought that his uncle might abandon him and that he would no longer have his support, but nevertheless he answered, 'O my uncle, by Allah, if they put the sun in my right hand and the moon in my left in return for my giving up this cause, I would not give it up until Allah makes Truth victorious, or I die in His service.'

Abū Ṭālib was deeply moved by this answer. He told the Prophet ﷺ that he would support him for as long as he lived and encouraged him to go on spreading Allah's message. From that time on, however hard the leaders of Quraysh tried to convince Abū Ṭālib to stop protecting his nephew, he always refused to listen to them.

In order to get rid of the Prophet ﷺ and his followers, his enemies started persecuting those Muslims who were poor or weak, or had no powerful friends. One such person was Bilāl, the slave of Umayyah ibn Khalaf. His master would take him out into the desert, tie him up, and leave him in the sun with a large stone on his chest. Fortunately Abū Bakr was passing by one day and saw Umayyah torturing Bilāl, so he bought him from his master for a large sum of money and then set him free.

But not all persecuted Muslims were as fortunate as Bilāl. Many suffered, but all of them endured it patiently, knowing that they were doing the right thing and that their reward in the life to come would be greater than any happiness they could find on earth.

THE KING WHO BELIEVED

As the number of the Prophet's followers increased so the enemies of the Muslims grew more and more angry. At last some of the Muslims decided to go to another country in order to live in peace. It was only five years since the Archangel Gabriel had first come to the Prophet ﷺ and two years since the Prophet ﷺ had spoken out in public. The Muslims asked the Prophet ﷺ to allow them to leave Mecca. He agreed, saying 'It would be better for you to go to Abyssinia. The king there is a just man and it is a friendly country. Stay there until Allah makes it possible for you to return.'

The Muslims prepared for the journey. They decided to wait until night so that they could leave without being seen. The first sixteen left Mecca and, after reaching the shore of the Red Sea, crossed over to Abyssinia. Another eighty-three men and nineteen women followed, all hoping to be welcomed by the king and people of that country. This was the first *hijrah*, or migration, in Islam.

The Meccans were furious when they discovered that these Muslims had secretly left the city for among them were the sons and daughters of many of the leading families of Mecca. The anger of the Meccans was even greater when they found out that the Muslims had been warmly welcomed in Abyssinia.

The leaders of Quraysh decided to send two men to the Abyssinian king in hopes of persuading him to send the Muslims back. These were ʿAmr ibn al-ʿĀṣ, a very clever speaker, and ʿAbd Allāh ibn abī Rabiʿah. Before they met this king, they gave each of his advisers a gift, saying: 'Some foolish men from our people have come to hide in your country. Our leaders have sent us to your ruler to persuade him to send them back, so when we speak to the king about them, do advise him to give them up to us.' The advisers agreed to do what the Meccans wished.

'Amr ibn al-'Āṣ and 'Abd Allāh ibn abī Rabi'ah then went to the king and presented him also with a gift, saying: 'Your Highness, these people have abandoned the religion we have always followed in Mecca, but they have not even become Christians like you.'

The royal advisers, who were also present, told the king that the Meccans had spoken the truth and that he should send the Muslims back to their own people. At this, the king became angry and said, 'No, by God, I will not give them up. Those who have come to ask for my protection, settled in my country, and chosen me rather than others, shall not be betrayed. I will summon them and ask them about what these two men have said. If the Muslims are as the Meccans say, I will give them up and send them back to their own people, but if the Meccans have lied I will protect the Muslims.'

'Amr was very upset by this for the last thing he wanted was for the king to hear what the Muslims had to say. The king then sent for the Muslims. When they entered, they did not kneel before him as was the custom of the Abyssinians.

'Why do you not kneel before our king?' they were asked by one of the advisors.

'We kneel only to Allah', they replied. So the king asked them to tell him about their religion.

Ja'far ibn abī Ṭālib, 'Alī's brother and a cousin of the Prophet ﷺ, was chosen to speak for the Muslims. He replied, 'O King, at first we were among the ignorant. We and our ancestors had turned from the faith of Abraham, who, with Ishmael, rebuilt the Ka'bah and worshipped only Allah. We used idols in our worship of Allah; we ate meat that had not been killed in the right way; we did not respect the rights of our neighbours; the strong took advantage of the weak. We did terrible things of which I dare not speak. This was our life until Allah sent a Messenger from among us, one of our relatives, whom we have always known to be honest, innocent, and faithful. He asked us to worship only Allah, and to give up the bad customs of our forefathers. He asked us to be truthful and trustworthy, to respect and help our neighbours, to honour our families, and to put a stop to our bad deeds and endless fighting. He asked us to look after orphans. He ordered us not to slander or speak evil of women or men. He ordered us to worship Allah alone and not to worship anyone or anything else alongside Him. He ordered us to pray, to give alms, and to fast. We believe he is right and therefore we follow him and do as he has commanded us. The Meccans began to attack us and come between us and our religion. So we had to leave our homes and we have come to you, hoping to find justice.'

The king, who was a Christian, was moved by these words. 'Amr had to think quickly of a way to win the argument. Cunningly he said to the king, 'These people do not believe in Jesus in the same way as you'. The king then wanted to know what the Prophet ﷺ had said about Jesus. Ja'far replied by reciting a *sūrah* from the Koran which tells the story of Jesus and his mother Mary. These are a few of the lines he recited:

In the Name of Allah, the Beneficent, the Merciful

And make mention of Mary in the Scripture, when she had withdrawn from her people to an eastern place, And had chosen seclusion from them. Then We sent unto her Our spirit and it assumed for her the likeness of a perfect man.
She said: Lo! I seek refuge in the Beneficent One from thee, if thou fearest God.
He said: I am only a messenger of thy Lord, that I may bestow on thee a faultless son.
She said: How can I have a son when no mortal hath touched me, neither have I been unchaste?
He said: 'Even so thy Lord saith: It is easy for Me. And (it will be) that We may make of him a revelation for mankind and a mercy from Us, and it is a thing ordained.
And she conceived him, and she withdrew with him to a far place.
Then she brought him to her own folk, carrying him. They said: O Mary! Thou hast come with an monstrous thing.
Oh sister of Aaron! Thy father was not a wicked man nor was thy mother a harlot.

Then Mary pointed to the child (Jesus);
But they said, 'How can we speak
to one who is still in the cradle,
  a young child?'
He said, 'Lo, I am Allah's servant;
He has given me the Book, and
  made me a Prophet.

He has made me Blessed, wheresoever
I may be; and He has enjoined me
to pray, and to give alms, so
long as I live,
and likewise to cherish my mother;
He has not made me arrogant,
unblest
Peace be upon me, the day I was born,
and the day I die, and the day I am
raised up alive!'

(*Koran* xix:16–33)

When the king heard this, his eyes filled with tears. Turning to his advisers, he said, 'These words have surely come from God; there is very little to separate the Muslims from the Christians. What both Jesus and Muḥammad, the Messengers of Allah, have brought comes from the same source.'

So the Muslims were given the king's permission to live peacefully in his country. ʿAmr was given back the gift he had presented to the king and the two Meccans returned home, bitterly disappointed.

THE CRUELTY OF QURAYSH

THE leaders of Quraysh became increasingly worried about the way the people of Mecca were being divided by the Prophet's teachings. Finally, 'Umar ibn al-Khaṭṭāb, one of the nobles of Mecca, decided that the only way to silence the Prophet ﷺ was to kill him. Having made up his mind, he set out at once to look for him.

On his way he met a man who saw at once what 'Umar was going to do and said: 'Why don't you look a little closer to home before going to kill Muḥammad? Don't you know your own sister Fāṭimah is a Muslim?'

'Umar was shocked. He could not believe this was true. He went at once to his sister's house. When he arrived outside the house he heard Fāṭimah and her husband Sa'īd reading aloud *sūrah* Ṭā Hā, a chapter from the Koran. Hearing her brother's voice at the door, Fāṭimah quickly hid the scroll with the *sūrah* written on it among the folds of her dress. 'Umar stormed into the room and demanded, 'What is this nonsense I heard?' Fāṭimah denied everything. 'Umar then lost his temper and attacked Fāṭimah's husband shouting, 'They tell me that you have joined Muḥammad in his religion!' Fāṭimah tried to defend her husband and 'Umar hit her too.

Then she admitted, 'Yes, we are Muslims and we believe in Allah and His Messenger and you can do what you like!'

Seeing her faith and courage, 'Umar suddenly felt sorry for what he had done and said to his sister, 'Let me see what I heard you reading just now so that I may understand just what it is that your Prophet has brought.'

Fāṭimah gave the scroll to him after he had washed to make himself clean and pure before touching it, and had promised to give it back to her afterwards.

In the Name of Allah, the Beneficent, the Merciful

Tā Hā
We have not revealed unto thee (Muḥammad) this Koran
For thee to be distressed, but only as a reminder
Unto him who fears, a Revelation from
Him who created the earth and the high heavens;
the Beneficent One
Who is established on the Throne;
To Him belongs
Whatsoever is in the heavens and the earth
And all that is between them, and
All that is underneath the soil.
If Thou speakest aloud
Be thou loud in thy speech, yet
Surely He knows the secret (thought)
And that yet more hidden.
Allah
There is no god but He
To Him belong the Most Beautiful Names.

(*Koran* xx:1–8)

As he read, 'Umar suddenly knew that these were the most beautiful words he had ever heard and that this religion must be the true one. With his sword still in hand, he went straight to the Prophet's house and knocked loudly at the door. One of the Prophet's closest followers looked out. There stood 'Umar who was known for his courage and strength. When he saw 'Umar so excited and with his sword in hand, he was afraid for the Prophet's life. But the Prophet ﷺ asked him to allow 'Umar to come in and to leave them alone together.

The Prophet ﷺ asked 'Umar why he had come, to which he replied: 'I have come to swear that there is no god but Allah and that you, Muḥammad, are the Messenger of Allah.' As he spoke these words, his hand still held the sword with which he had intended to kill the Prophet ﷺ. This same sword would now be used to defend the Prophet ﷺ and the faith of Islam.

At that time, whenever Muslims wanted to perform the ritual encircling of the Ka'bah, known as *tawaf*, they had to do it secretly and in fear. 'Umar, however, was very courageous. As soon as he had declared his faith, he went directly to the Ka'bah and in broad daylight made the circling of the Sacred House before the astonished people of Mecca. No one dared to say anything. But now the leaders of Quraysh became even more alarmed and began to see Islam as a threat to the whole life of the city of Mecca. They grew more and more furious as the numbers of Muslims increased until finally they, too, decided as 'Umar once had, that the Prophet ﷺ would have to be killed.

On hearing of these plans, Abū Ṭālib, the Prophet's uncle, immediately sent a message to all the sons of 'Abd al-Muṭṭalib, asking them to protect their nephew, and this they agreed to do. When Quraysh realised that they could not kill the Prophet ﷺ because of this protection, they decided instead to avoid him and his followers completely. A declaration to this effect was hung at the Ka'bah. It stated that no one in the city was allowed to have anything to do with the Prophet ﷺ and his people, or even to sell them any food or drink whatsoever.

At first the Muslims found some support among the Banī Hāshim, the branch of Quraysh to which the Prophet ﷺ belonged. Some of these people were not Muslims but showed loyalty to their kinsmen by suffering along with them. However, life grew more and more difficult and food was scarce. The hatred of the rest of Quraysh for the followers of the Prophet ﷺ grew so great that when his companions tried to buy supplies from a caravan passing near to Mecca, Abū Lahab, one of the Muslims' worst enemies, offered ten times the price of the goods to the merchant. By doing this he managed to stop the Muslims from buying what they desperately needed.

During the years of this terrible treatment, a wonderful thing happened. Instead of Islam becoming weaker, it grew stronger. Allah sent more and more Revelations. It was as though the Muslims were being strengthened and cleansed by the hardships they suffered and were being tested in their faith.

Each year, at the time of the pilgrimage to Mecca, people came from all over Arabia. These pilgrims saw the terrible cruelty and injustice of Quraysh towards the Muslims, and many of them were sorry for the Prophet's followers. Quraysh began to feel ashamed of their harsh treatment, especially as many of the Muslims were their cousins and close relatives.

Finally, at the end of three years, they were convinced that the time had come to put an end to the persecution of the Muslims, and they decided to take down the notice hanging at the Ka'bah. To their astonishment, the sheet of paper had been completely eaten up by worms, all except the words, 'In Your Name, O Allah', which had been written at the top of the paper.

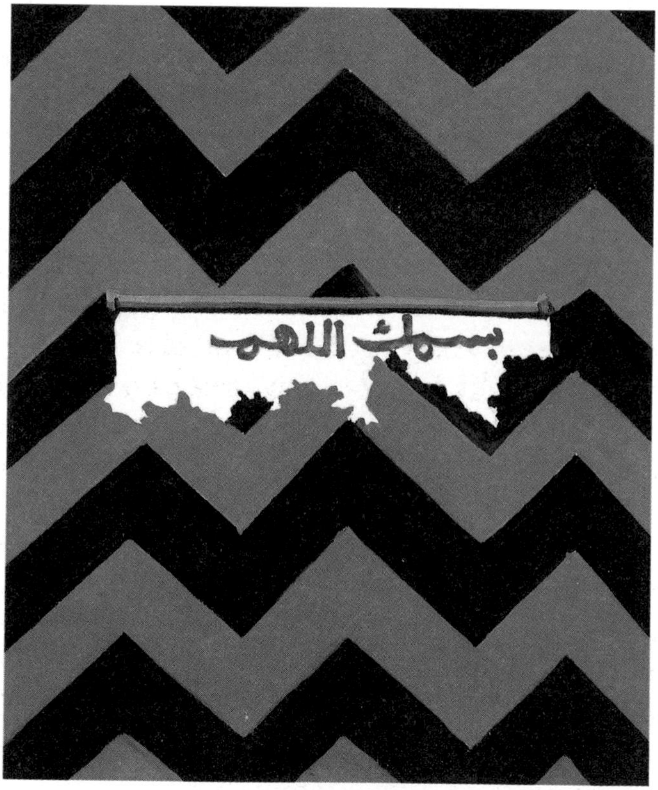

THE YEAR OF SORROW

THE Prophet ﷺ and his followers went back to a normal way of life but the years of hardship had made Khadījah very weak. She became ill and soon afterwards she died. Thus, the Prophet ﷺ lost his beloved wife and friend, the first person to accept Islam and support him. She had been a refuge from all his troubles and, through her good-heartedness, the best company in his suffering. He had loved her very much. This happened in 619 A.D., the year which became known as the 'Year of Sorrow'.

Soon after this, the Prophet Muḥammad's uncle and protector, Abū Ṭālib, also died. Abū Ṭālib had been one of the most respected men in Mecca—one of the elders of Quraysh. Even though he had never been a follower of Islam, he had protected the Prophet ﷺ against his enemies. Not only was this a sad occasion for the Prophet ﷺ but also a dangerous one. According to Arab custom anyone who is under the protection of another is safe so long as his protector lives. Now, with the death of his uncle, the Prophet's protection was gone.

The Prophet's enemies rejoiced to see him so sad, without a wife to console and comfort him, and without his uncle to protect him. They began to treat him worse than ever before. Even small children insulted him. One young man actually threw some filth on the Prophet's head, but the Prophet ﷺ went home without making anything of it. When one of his daughters rushed, weeping, to wash it away, he comforted her saying, 'Do not weep my little girl, for Allah will protect your father.'

Abū Ṭālib had been the Prophet's last tie with Quraysh and the Prophet ﷺ now felt that Islam could make no further progress in Mecca because the hearts of Quraysh were closed against him. He decided, therefore, to travel to

Ṭā'if where he hoped to find support. He walked all the way to the town, which was seventy kilometres away. There he spoke in all the places where people gathered, but no one listened to him. He met the leaders of the three most important tribes but they would not listen either. Not only did they take no notice of what he said, but they laughed at him and ordered their slaves to insult him and pelt him with stones.

Sadly, the Prophet ﷺ left the city and found a quiet place near a wall on the edge of town where he could be alone. There he prayed to Allah in these words:

> O Allah, to Thee I complain of my weakness, helplessness and lowliness before men. O Most Merciful, Thou art the Lord of the weak, and Thou art my Lord. To whom wouldst Thou leave my fate? To a stranger who insults me or to an enemy to whom Thou hast given power over me? If Thou art not angry with me, I care not what happens to me. Thy favour alone is my objective. I take refuge in the Light of Thy countenance by which the darkness is illumined and on which this world and the other depend, lest Thy anger descend upon me or Thy wrath light upon me. It is for Thee to be satisfied until Thou art well pleased. There is no power and no might save through Thee.

The wall near which the Prophet ﷺ was sitting belonged to a garden owned by two brothers. When they heard his prayer, they were very sorry for him and sent one of their slaves to him with a dish filled with grapes. Before he began to eat, the Prophet ﷺ said 'Bismillah'—'In the Name of Allah.' The servant, whose name was 'Addās, was very surprised at these words, which he had never heard before.

'By Allah', said 'Addās, 'this is not the way the people of this country speak.'

'Then from what country do you come, 'Addās, and what is your religion?' asked the Prophet ﷺ.

'I am a Christian from the Assyrian town of Nineveh', he replied.

'From the town of that good man Jonah, son of Matta', added the Prophet ﷺ.

'How do you know about him?' asked 'Addās.

'He is my brother—he was a Prophet and I am a Prophet', answered the Messenger of Allah ﷺ.

'Addās bent down and kissed the Prophet's head, his hands and his feet, because now he saw that he was truly a Prophet.

The Prophet ﷺ then walked back to Mecca. He was now able to put up with everything patiently for he knew that Allah would never leave him. His journey to Ṭā'if had not been in vain for 'Addās, the Christian, had become a Muslim, and this was to be the beginning of great changes.

THE NIGHT JOURNEY AND THE ASCENT TO HEAVEN

ONE night as the Prophet ﷺ lay sleeping in the same spot where 'Abd al-Muṭṭalib used to sleep, next to the Ka'bah, he was woken by the Archangel Gabriel. Later the Prophet ﷺ described what happened: 'I sat up and he took hold of my arm. I stood beside him and he brought me to the door of the mosque where there was a white animal for me to ride.'

The Prophet ﷺ told of how he mounted the animal and, with the Archangel Gabriel at his side, was transported from Mecca to the mosque called al-Aqsa, in far away Jerusalem. There the Prophet ﷺ found Abraham, Moses, and Jesus among a group of Prophets. The Prophet Muḥammad ﷺ acted as their leader, or imam, in prayer. Then he was brought two jugs, one containing wine and the other milk. He chose the milk and refused the wine. At this, the Archangel Gabriel said, 'You have been rightly guided to the *fitrah*, the true nature of man, and so will your people be, Muḥammad. Wine is forbidden to you.'

The Prophet ﷺ also related how they passed through Heaven's gates and saw countless angels. Among them was Malik, the Keeper of Hell, who never smiles. Malik stepped forward and showed the Prophet ﷺ a view of Hell and the terrible plight of those who suffer in that place.

Then the Prophet ﷺ was taken up by the angels, through the seven Heavens, one by one. Along the way he again saw Jesus, Moses, and Abraham, and the Prophet ﷺ said that he had never seen a man more like himself than Abraham. He also saw John, called Yahya in Arabic, Joseph or Yusef, Enoch, that is Idris, and Aaron.

At last he reached the Lote Tree of the Uttermost, the *sidrat al-muntaha*, where no Prophet had been before. Here the Prophet ﷺ received a Revelation of what Muslims believe.

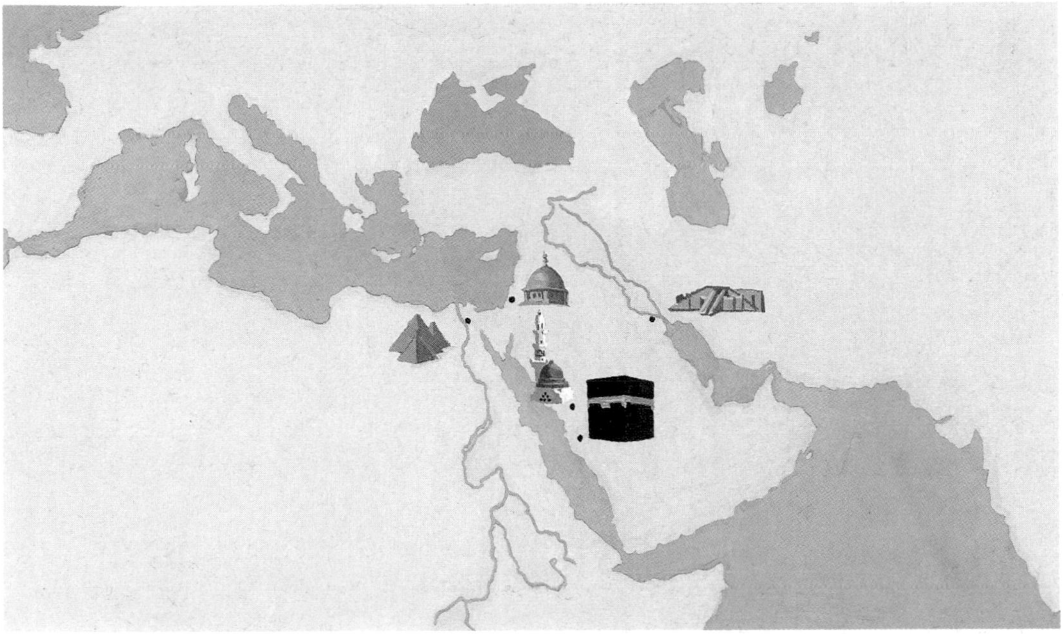

In the Name of Allah, the Beneficent, the Merciful

The Messenger believeth in that which hath been revealed unto him from his Lord and (so do) the believers. Each one believes in Allah and His Angels and His Books and His Messengers—We make no distinction between any of His messengers—and they say: We hear, and we obey. Grant us Thy forgiveness, our Lord. Unto Thee is the homecoming.

(*Koran* ii.285)

Then he was taken into the Light of the Divine Presence of Allah, and was instructed that Muslims should pray fifty times a day. The Prophet ﷺ recalled:

> On my way back I passed by Moses and what a good friend to you he was! He asked me how many prayers had I been ordained to perform. When I told him fifty, he said, 'Prayer is a serious matter and your people are weak, so go back to your Lord and ask Him to reduce the number for you and your community.' I did so and He took away ten. Again I passed by Moses and he said the same again; and so it went on until only five prayers for the whole day

and night were left. Moses again gave me the same advice. I replied that I had been back to my Lord and asked him to reduce the number until I was ashamed, and I would not do it again. He of you who performs the five prayers faithfully, will have the reward of fifty prayers.

On the morning following these events and the Prophet's return to Mecca, he told Quraysh what had happened. Most of them said, 'By God! This is ridiculous! A caravan takes a month to go to Syria and a month to return! Can you do that long journey in a single night?'

Even many Muslims were amazed by this and wanted the Prophet ﷺ to explain. Some ran with the news to Abū Bakr who said, 'By Allah, if Muḥammad ﷺ himself has said so, then it is true. Remember, the Prophet tells us that the word of Allah comes to him directly from heaven to earth at any hour by day or night, and we believe him. Isn't that a greater miracle than what you are now doubting?'

Then Abū Bakr went to the mosque and listened to the Prophet's detailed description of Jerusalem. He commented, 'You tell the truth, O Prophet of Allah!' From then on, Abū Bakr was honoured with the title 'al-Ṣiddiq', which means 'he who gives his word to support the truth'.

Others also began to believe the Prophet's story when he went on to describe two caravans he had seen on his way back to Mecca. He told the doubters where he had seen the caravans, what they were carrying and when they would arrive in Mecca. All that the Prophet ﷺ had said was borne out when the caravans arrived at the time he said they would, carrying all that he had described.

In the Name of Allah, the Beneficent, the Merciful

Glory be to Him, who carried His servant by night
from the Holy Mosque to the Far distant place of worship,
the Neighbourhood which We have blessed,
that We might show him some of Our signs,
He, only He is the All-hearing, the All-seeing.

(*Koran* xvii: 1)

By the Star when it setteth,
Your comrade is not astray, neither deceived,
Nor does he speak of his (own) desire.
This is naught but a revelation revealed,
Taught him by one mighty in power, very strong;
he stood poised,
being on the uppermost horizon,
Then drew near and came down,
two bows'-length away, or nearer,
Then revealed to His servant that which He revealed.
His heart lies not of what he saw;
What, will you then dispute with him what he sees?
Indeed, he saw him yet another time
By the Lote-Tree of the utmost Boundary
Near which is the Garden of Abode
When there covered the Lote-Tree that which covered;
his eye turned not aside, nor yet was overbold.
Verily, he saw one of the greatest signs of his Lord.

(*Koran* liii: 1–18)

THE TREATY OF 'AQABAH

In Yathrib there were two main tribes, the Aws and the Khazraj. Both were very powerful, they were always at war with one another, and both worshipped idols. Also in Yathrib were many Jews who, unlike the Arabs at that time, knew that there was only One God, and worshipped Him. They had told the Arabs many times that a Prophet would be coming to them.

The time came for the pilgrimage to the Ka'bah, and several people from Yathrib were going, among them six men from the tribe of Khazraj. They had heard about the Prophet Muḥammad's preaching and thought that this must be the Prophet the Jews had told them about. So they decided to go and speak to him during their stay in Mecca.

They met the Prophet ﷺ at a spot known as 'Aqabah, near Mecca, and he invited them to sit with him. He explained to them what Islam meant and recited to them from the Koran. When they heard the Koran recited it touched their hearts so deeply that they became Muslims and on leaving Mecca they promised to return the following year. When they reached Yathrib carrying Islam in their hearts, they told their relatives and friends what they had heard from the Prophet ﷺ and many more people became Muslims.

A year passed and the pilgrimage season came around again. Twelve important men from Yathrib went to Mecca to meet the Prophet ﷺ and promised faithfully to serve him and Islam. In return, the Prophet ﷺ sent one of his friends, Muṣ'ab ibn 'Umayr, with them to teach the Koran and instruct them in their new religion.

Another year passed and still more Muslims came from Yathrib to Mecca for the pilgrimage. On this occasion a secret meeting with the Prophet ﷺ was arranged to be held at night. Seventy-three men and one woman from

Yathrib came, and the Prophet ﷺ arrived with his uncle, al-'Abbās. During this meeting the men from Yathrib offered to protect and defend the Prophet ﷺ and his followers if they would come to live in Yathrib. This promise of protection came to be known as the Treaty of 'Aqabah.

The treaty was most fortunate for even though Islam was growing in Yathrib, the Muslims in Mecca were still suffering. The Prophet ﷺ therefore told his friends and followers to go to Yathrib where they would be safe, and most of them took this opportunity to leave.

Despite all this suffering the Prophet ﷺ was not allowed to fight his enemies, for Allah had told him to forgive those who insulted him or would not listen to his message. But the Quraysh had closed their minds so utterly to the word of Allah, and grew so hard-hearted towards the Prophet ﷺ and his followers, that Allah gave permission to the Prophet ﷺ to fight those who tried to harm him or his companions.

In the Name of Allah, the Beneficent, the Merciful

Permission is given unto those who
fight because they have been wronged;
And Allah is surely able to give
them victory;
Those who have been driven from
their homes unjustly only because they
said: Our Lord is Allah.

(*Koran* xxii.39–40)

Quraysh began to fear the Prophet ﷺ for they realised that he was now strong enough to fight them and had been given leave to do so by Allah. They also knew that he now had the people of Yathrib to help and protect him. Seeing that the Muslims were leaving the city, they decided to kill the Prophet ﷺ, before he, too, left Mecca to join his followers in Yathrib. In this way they hoped to put an end to Islam once and for all.

AL-HIJRAH

*The Breaking of All Connections with One's Home,
for the Sake of Allah Alone*

AFTER his companions had left for Yathrib, the Prophet ﷺ stayed in Mecca, waiting for permission from Allah to leave the city. Abū Bakr and 'Alī stayed with him. There were also some Muslims whom Quraysh had not allowed to leave. Abū Bakr kept asking the Prophet ﷺ to allow him to go to Yathrib, but the Messenger of Allah ﷺ kept saying, 'Do not be in a hurry; it might be that Allah will give you a travelling companion.'

The leaders of Quraysh assembled in the house of their ancestor, Quṣayy, as was customary when they had an important decision to make. They had to find a way of getting rid of the Prophet Muḥammad ﷺ, before he was able to join his friends in Yathrib.

As they were busy arguing, the Devil appeared at the door in the form of a noble and handsome old man. When they saw this elderly gentleman standing there, they asked him who he was. He said he was a sheikh from the mountains who had heard what they meant to do and thought he might be able to help or advise them. They thought he looked like a wise man, so they invited him in.

Each leader then started to put forward ideas about what should be done, but none of them could agree about which was best, until Abū Jahl told them his plan. This was that each clan should provide a strong, young warrior, each of whom would be given a sword. All the young warriors would then wait outside the Prophet's house and together attack him as he came out. In this way they would be rid of him but as the blame for killing him would fall on all the clans, the Prophet's family would not be able to seek revenge.

When he heard this, the Devil in the disguise of the old man, said, 'That man is right; in my opinion it is the only thing to do!' The leaders of Quraysh then left to carry out their plan to murder the Prophet ﷺ.

In the Name of Allah, the Beneficent, the Merciful

And when the unbelievers plot
against thee, to confine thee, or kill thee,
or to drive thee out, they were plotting,
But Allah was (also) plotting; and Allah is
the best of plotters. (*Koran* viii.30)

Before the night fell, on which Muḥammad ﷺ was to be killed, the Archangel Gabriel came to him and said, 'Do not sleep tonight in your own bed.' The Prophet ﷺ understood what was going to happen, so he told 'Alī to lie in his bed and wrap himself in the blanket that the Prophet ﷺ normally used, promising that no harm would befall him.

With the coming of darkness the young men of Quraysh had gathered outside the Prophet's house, waiting for him to come out. After he had made sure that 'Alī was safe, the Prophet ﷺ left the house. At that very moment, Allah took away the sight of the warriors so that they could not see the Prophet ﷺ, who took a handful of dust, sprinkled it on their heads and recited these verses:

In the Name of Allah, the Beneficent, the Merciful

Ya Sīn
By the Wise Koran,
Thou art truly among those sent
On the straight path;
A Revelation of the All-mighty, the All-wise,
That thou may warn a people whose fathers were
never warned, so they are heedless.
The Word has already proved true of most of them,
yet they do not believe.
Lo! We have put on their necks collars of iron
up to the chin, so that they are made stiff-necked.
And We have put before them a barrier; and We have
covered them so they do not see. (*Koran* xxxvi.1–9)

The young men waited the whole night and were furious when, in the morning, they saw 'Alī instead of the Prophet ﷺ coming out of the house. They realised that their plan had failed completely.

In the meantime, the Prophet ﷺ went to Abū Bakr's house and told him, 'Allah has told me that now is the time for us to leave Mecca.'

'Together?' asked Abū Bakr.

'Together', the Prophet ﷺ replied.

Abū Bakr wept for joy, because now he knew that the travelling companion he had been promised was the Prophet ﷺ himself. Then he said, 'O Messenger of Allah, these are the two camels which I have kept ready for this.' And so, the two of them left for a cave in Thawr, a mountain to the south of Mecca where they intended to hide.

When they were out of the city the Prophet ﷺ looked back and said, 'Of all Allah's earth, you are the dearest place to Allah and to me and if my people had not driven me out I would never have left you.'

When Quraysh found out that the Prophet ﷺ and his companion had gone, they set out after them, searching in every direction. Three days later they finally reached the cave where the Prophet ﷺ and Abū Bakr were hiding, but a strange and wonderful thing had happened. A spider had woven its web right across the entrance to the cave and a dove was nesting with her mate nearby. As the Meccans stood in front of the cave, with only the spider's web separating them from the fugitives, Abū Bakr began to fear for their safety. He whispered to the Prophet ﷺ, 'They are very close. If one of them turns we will be seen.'

But he was comforted by the Prophet's reply: 'What do you think of two people, who have with them Allah as their third?'

Grieve not, for verily Allah is with us. (*Koran* ix.40)

After a few moments the search party decided that no one could have entered the cave recently, or the spider's web would not have been complete and the dove would not have nested there, and so they left without searching inside.

Three days later the Prophet ﷺ and Abū Bakr thought it safe to leave the cave. Abū Bakr's son, 'Amir, had arranged for three camels and a guide to help them continue their journey to Yathrib. 'Amir would ride behind his father.

The leaders of Quraysh, meanwhile, returned to Mecca and offered a reward of one hundred camels to whoever captured the Prophet ﷺ. Among those who went in search of him was a famous warrior. He was, in fact, the only one to catch up with him, but whenever he came close, his horse would suddenly sink up to its knees in the sand. When this had happened three times, he understood that the Prophet ﷺ was protected by a power stronger than anything he had known, and so he went back to Mecca. On arriving there he warned everyone against continuing the search, relating what had happened to him.

In the Name of Allah, the Beneficent, the Merciful

If you do not help him, still Allah has helped him already,
When the unbelievers drove him forth, the second of two,
When the two were in the Cave,
when he said to his companion, "Grieve not; surely Allah is with us."
Then Allah caused His peace and Reassurance to descend upon him,
And helped him with hosts you cannot see,
And He made the word of the unbelievers the lowest;
While Allah's word is the uppermost;
Allah is All-mighty, All-wise.

(*Koran* ix.40)

The Prophet's journey from Mecca is called the *ḥijrah*, or migration. It was really the first step towards the spread of Islam throughout the entire world, and Muslims begin their calendar from the year of the *ḥijrah*.

ARRIVAL IN YATHRIB

WHEN the people of Yathrib heard that the Prophet ﷺ had left Mecca and was on his way to their city, they anxiously awaited his arrival. Each morning they would go to the edge of the city to see if he were coming. Finally, on Monday, September 27, in the year 622 A.D., someone saw him in the distance and shouted to everyone, 'Here is Muḥammad! ﷺ the Messenger of Allah has arrived!' All the Muslims went out to greet him, shouting, 'Allāhu Akbar! Allah is Great! Muḥammad the Messenger of Allah has arrived!' The women and children sang songs to show how glad they were to see him.

The Prophet ﷺ entered the city with his friend Abū Bakr. Most of the people there had not seen him before and as they gathered around they did not know which of the two was the Prophet ﷺ, until Abū Bakr got up to shield him with his cloak from the burning sun. Yathrib would now be called al-Medina, which means, The City.

The Messenger of God ﷺ stayed in Qubā', which is a place at the entrance of Medina, for three days. On the first Friday after his arrival the Prophet ﷺ led the congregation in prayer. After this many of the wealthiest men invited him to come and live with them and share their riches. But he refused and, pointing to his she-camel, Qaṣwā', said, 'Let her go her way', because he knew that his camel was under Allah's command and would guide him to the spot where he should stay. They let the camel go until she finally knelt down beside a house belonging to the Bani an-Najjār, the tribe to whom the Prophet's mother was related. This house was used as a drying-place for dates and belonged to two young orphan boys named Sahl and Suhayl. They offered to give it to the Prophet ﷺ but he insisted on paying them for it, and so their guardian, As'ad the son of Zurārah, who was present, made the necessary arrangements.

The Prophet ﷺ ordered that a mosque and a place for him to live be built on the site. All the Muslims worked together to finish it quickly—even the Prophet ﷺ joined in. It was here that the Muslims would pray and meet to make important decisions and plans. The building was quite plain and simple. The floor was beaten earth and the roof of palm leaves was held up by tree trunks. Two stones marked the direction of prayer. At first worshippers faced Jerusalem, but soon after the direction of prayer was changed towards the Kaʿbah in Mecca.

After the building of the mosque, the Prophet ﷺ wanted to strengthen the relationship between the people called the Muhājirah or Emigrants, who had left Mecca with him, and the people of Medina, who were known as the Anṣār, or Helpers. Each man from Medina took as his brother a man from Mecca, sharing everything with him and treating him as a member of his own family. This was the beginning of the Islamic brotherhood.

In the early days of Islam, the times for prayer were not announced and so the Muslims would come to the mosque and wait for the prayer so as not to miss it. The Prophet ﷺ wondered how to tell the people that it was time for prayers. He discussed it with his friends, and at first two ideas were put forward; that of blowing a horn as the Jews did, and that of using a wooden clapper like the Christians. Then a man called ʻAbd Allāh ibn Zayd came to the Prophet ﷺ and told him he had had a dream in which he had seen a man dressed all in green, holding a wooden clapper. He had said to the man, 'Would you sell me your clapper in order to call the people to prayer?' The man had replied, 'A better way to call the people to prayer is to say:

> "Allāhu Akbar, Allah is Most Great!" four times, followed by
> "I bear witness that there is no divinity but Allah,
> I bear witness that Muḥammad is the Messenger of Allah,
> Come to prayer, come to prayer,
> Come to salvation, come to salvation.
> Allāhu Akbar, Allāhu Akbar!
> There is no divinity but Allah!"'

When the Prophet ﷺ heard this, he said it was a true vision from Allah. He sent for Bilāl, who had a beautiful, strong voice, and ordered him to call the people to prayer in just this way. Bilāl did so and soon after ʻUmar came out of his house and told the Prophet ﷺ that he had seen exactly the same vision himself. The Prophet ﷺ replied, 'Allah be praised for that.'

The *adhān*, or call to prayer, which came to ʻAbd Allāh ibn Zayd in his dream and was performed by Bilāl on the instruction of the Prophet ﷺ, is the one we still hear today being called from the minarets of mosques all over the world.

THE BATTLE OF BADR

THE Muslims who had gone to Medina, had left all their belongings behind in Mecca and these had been taken by their enemies. Thus, when the Muslims heard that Abū Sufyān, one of the leaders of Quraysh, was on his way back to Mecca from Syria with a large caravan of goods, they decided that the time had come for them to retrieve some of their losses. The Prophet ﷺ gave the Muslims permission for this attack and everyone began to get ready for the raid, for it had been revealed:

In the Name of Allah, the Beneficent, the Merciful

Permission to fight is given unto those who fight because
they have been wronged; and Allah is surely able
to give them victory;

(*Koran* xxii.39)

The Revelation had mentioned that a thing most serious with Allah was

to turn (men) from the way of Allah, and to
disbelieve in Him and in the Holy Mosque, and
to drive his people from there . . . for persecution
is worse than killing.

(*Koran* ii.217)

The retrieval of their goods, however, was not their only reason for wanting to attack the caravan. The Muslims did not think they should simply remain safely in Medina; they wanted to spread the message of Islam. They thus felt that if Quraysh wanted freedom to trade in safety, then the Muslims must also have freedom to believe in Allah, to follow His Messenger ﷺ, and spread His Word. It was, therefore, thought that the best, and only way to get Quraysh to understand this was to attack what was most important to them—a caravan.

Abū Sufyān, in the meantime, heard about the Muslims' plan and quickly sent a message to Quraysh in Mecca, telling them that the caravan was in danger and asking for help. As a result nearly all Quraysh came out to help him defend the caravan. There were a thousand men and two hundred horses. The women also went along to cheer the men on with their singing.

Unaware of this, the Prophet ﷺ set out with his followers. It was the month of Ramadan and the Muslims were fasting. There were only three hundred and five of them, most of them Anṣār, men from Medina. With them they had three horses and seventy camels, on which they rode in turns.

They arrived in the area of Badr, some distance from Medina where they made camp and waited for news of the caravan. Then they heard that Quraysh had set out from Mecca with a strong army. The situation had suddenly changed. They were no longer going to make a raid on a caravan—they were going to have to fight Quraysh.

The Prophet ﷺ gathered his men around him to find out what they wanted to do. First Abū Bakr, and then 'Umar, spoke for the Muslims who had come from Mecca. They said they would obey the Prophet ﷺ. But the Prophet ﷺ wanted to hear the opinion of the Anṣār, because he did not want to force them into doing something they did not want to do.

Sa'd ibn Mu'ādh, one of the leaders of the Anṣār, got up and said, 'We believe in you and we swear before all men that what you have brought is the truth. We have given you our word and agreement to hear and obey. So go where you wish, we are with you even if you should lead us into the sea!'

The Prophet ﷺ was greatly encouraged by these words and so it was agreed to fight.

Abū Sufyān learned where the Muslims were camped. He changed the course of the caravan and quickly took it out of their reach. He then sent word to Quraysh telling them that the caravan was safe and that they should return to Mecca. But the leaders of Quraysh were proud and stubborn men. They refused to return as they had made up their minds to show everyone how powerful they were by destroying the Muslims.

Now there was a *wādi*, or valley, at Badr, with wells on the side nearest Medina, and it was here that the Muslims took up position facing the valley with the wells behind them. Quraysh meanwhile placed themselves on the other side of the valley. The Muslims then dug a reservoir, filled it with water from one of the wells, and made a barrier around it. Then they stopped up the wells. In this way the Muslims had enough drinking water for themselves, while the Meccans would have to cross the valley and fight the Muslims in order to get water.

The night before the battle, while the Muslims slept peacefully, a heavy rain fell.

> *In the Name of Allah, the Beneficent, the Merciful*
> *When He made the slumber fall upon you as a reassurance from Him and sent down water from the sky upon you, in order that He might purify you, and remove from you the fear of Satan, and strengthen your hearts and make firm (your) feet thereby.*
>
> (*Koran* viii.11)

On the morning of Friday, the 17th of Ramadan, 2 A.H., (March 17th, 623 A.D.), the two armies advanced and drew closer to one another. The rain had been heavier on the side of Quraysh, making the ground soft and movement difficult. On the side of the Muslims, however, the rain had packed the sand down hard, making it easy for them to march. The Prophet ﷺ preferred the men to fight in ranks. As they prepared to march he noticed that someone had stepped out in front of the others. The Prophet ﷺ prodded him in the side with an arrow, saying, 'Stand in line!'

The man, Sawād, exclaimed, 'You have hurt me, O Messenger of Allah! Allah has sent you to be just and good.'

The Prophet ﷺ lifted his shirt and said, 'Then do the same to me.'

The man approached and kissed him on the spot instead, saying, 'O Messenger of Allah, you see what is before us and I may not survive the battle. If this is my last time with you, I want the last thing I do in life to be this.' Shortly after he went into battle, Sawād died a martyr.

Having examined the ranks, the Prophet ﷺ then went to a shelter made of palm branches from which he could command the battle. Abū Bakr stayed with him, while Sa'd ibn Mu'ādh, with several of the Anṣār, stood outside guarding the hut. When the Prophet ﷺ saw the enormous Quraysh army descending the hill into the valley, with all their banners and drums, he began to pray for the help which Allah had promised him. These were some of his words. 'O Allah, here come Quraysh full of vanity and pride, who oppose Thee and call Thy Messenger a liar. O Allah, if this little band (the Muslims) perishes today, there will be none left in the land to worship Thee.'

In the Name of Allah, the Beneficent, the Merciful

When ye sought help of your Lord and He answered you (saying): I will help you with a thousand of the angels, rank on rank.
Allah appointed it only as good tidings, and that your hearts might thereby be at ease. Victory cometh only by the help of Allah. Lo! Allah is Mighty, Wise.

(*Koran* viii.9–10)

At first the battle began in single combat when one of Quraysh swore that he would drink from the Muslims' reservoir and then destroy it, or die in the attempt. Ḥamzah, the Prophet's uncle, came forward to face him and killed him. Three of the most important men of Quraysh then stepped forward and gave out a challenge for single combat. The Prophet ﷺ sent out 'Alī, Ḥamzah, and 'Ubaydah ibn al-Ḥārith, to face them. It was not long before Ḥamzah and 'Alī had killed their opponents. As for 'Ubaydah, he had wounded his enemy but was wounded himself, and so his two companions killed the wounded Meccan and carried 'Ubaydah back to the safety of the Muslim ranks.

After this, the two armies attacked each other and fighting broke out all around. The sky was filled with arrows. The Muslim army held its ground against the great army of Quraysh and even though the Muslims were much fewer in number, they gained a great victory, destroying the Meccan army and killing most of its leaders. Among the leading Meccans who died were Abū Jahl and Umayyah ibn Khalaf, who was killed by his former slave, Bilāl. Seeing that their leaders were nearly all dead, the remainder of Quraysh retreated.

The Prophet ﷺ sent word to Medina to tell them of the victory. He then gathered up the spoils of war and divided them equally among the Muslims. Some of the Meccans had been taken prisoner and the Prophet ﷺ gave orders that they should be treated well until their relatives from among Quraysh came to fetch them.

In the Name of Allah, the Beneficent, the Merciful

Ye (Muslims) did not slay them, but Allah
slew them. And thou (Muḥammad) threwest not
when thou didst throw, but Allah threw, so that
He might test the believers by a fair test
from Him. Lo! Allah is All-hearing,
All-Knowing.

(*Koran* viii.17)

UHUD—DEFEAT COMES FROM DISOBEDIENCE

WHEN the survivors of the defeated Quraysh at Badr returned to Mecca, they gathered to speak with Abū Sufyān. They said, 'Muḥammad has killed our best men, so help us to fight him so that we may avenge those we have lost.' In order to do this it was agreed that everyone who had had a share in the caravan should put his profits towards the cost of a new army, which would be three times as big as the one at Badr.

Among those who joined the new army was an Abyssinian slave called Waḥshī, who was known for his accuracy with the spear. His master, Jubayr ibn al-Muṭ'im, said to him, 'Go with the army and if you kill Ḥamzah, the uncle of Muḥammad, in revenge for my uncle's death, I will set you free.' When Hind, Abū Sufyān's wife, heard about this she sent a message to Waḥshī to say that she would clothe him in gold and silk if he would carry out his master's wish, for she, too, wanted Ḥamzah dead because he had killed both her father and brother.

While the Meccans made their plans, the Prophet's uncle, 'Abbās, one of the few Muslims still living in Mecca, sent a letter of warning to the Prophet ﷺ in Medina. He told him that Quraysh were setting out with a huge army for Uhud, a place just outside Medina. On receiving this timely warning, the Prophet ﷺ gathered his companions around him to discuss what they should do. He thought it would be better to wait for the enemy inside the city rather than go out to meet them, because it would be easier to defend Medina from inside the city walls. But the young Muslims were eager to go out and face Quraysh. They said, 'O Prophet of Allah, lead us out against our enemies, or else they will think we are too cowardly and too weak to fight them.'

One of the rulers of Medina, 'Abd Allāh ibn Ubayy, however, agreed with the Prophet ﷺ and advised him to remain in the city, saying, 'Whenever we have gone out to fight an enemy we have met with disaster, but none has ever come in against us without being defeated.'

But when the Prophet ﷺ saw that the majority were in favour of going out to meet Quraysh, he decided to do so, and after the Friday prayer he put on his armour. The Muslims then set out with one thousand men in the direction of Mount Uhud which overlooks Medina. The enemy was camped on the plain below the mountain where they were laying waste the crops of the Muslims.

'Abd Allāh ibn Ubayy was angry that the Prophet ﷺ had not followed his advice and after going part of the way, turned back for Medina, taking one third of the entire army with him. This left the Prophet ﷺ with only seven hundred men to meet the enormous Meccan army, which numbered three thousand.

The remainder of the Muslims went on until they reached the mountain of Uhud. There the Prophet ﷺ ordered them to stand in ranks in front of the mountain, so that they would be protected from behind. He then positioned fifty archers on top of the mountain, giving them the following order: 'Keep the Meccan cavalry away from us with your arrows and don't let them come against us from the rear, whether the battle goes in our favour or against us. Whatever happens keep to your places so that we cannot be attacked from your direction, even if you see us being slain or booty being taken.'

When the Muslims were in position, the Prophet ﷺ held up his sword and said, 'Who will use this sword with its right?' This was a great honour and many men rose to claim it, but the Prophet ﷺ decided to give it to Abū Dujānah, a fearless warrior. Then the battle commenced.

The Muslims were well organized and had the advantage, because although Quraysh had more than four times as many men, they were tired from their journey and thus not ready to fight. As a result, the Muslims were able to make a surprise attack, led by Abū Dujānah, who was wearing a brilliant red turban.

As the fighting increased the Quraysh women, led by Hind, began to beat their drums to urge their men on. They called out poems to encourage their men to be brave.

'If you advance, we hug you,
spread soft rugs beneath you;
if you retreat, we leave you.
Leave and no more love you.'

Abū Dujānah said: 'I saw someone urging the enemy on, shouting wildly, and I made for him, but when I lifted my sword against him he screamed and I saw that it was a woman; I respected the Apostle's sword too much to use it on a woman.' That woman was Hind.

As usual, Ḥamzah, the Prophet's uncle, fought with great courage, but while leading the Muslims in a fierce attack, which nearly defeated the Meccans, he was suddenly and cruelly struck down by the slave Waḥshī. Later, Waḥshī told how it happened: 'I was watching Ḥamzah while he was killing men with his sword. I . . . aimed my spear until I was sure it would hit the mark and hurled it at him. He came on towards me but collapsed and fell. I left him there until he died, then I came and took back my spear. Then I went back to the camp because I did not want to kill anyone but him. My only aim in killing him was to gain my freedom.'

The Quraysh warriors were soon scattered and forced to retreat. It looked as though they had been defeated! Seeing this, forty of the fifty Muslim archers on top of the mountain ran down from their position to collect booty, for the Quraysh army had left many of their belongings behind. The archers rushed to take what they could, forgetting the Prophet's orders.

Khālid ibn al-Walīd, Commander of the Quraysh cavalry, saw what was happening and quickly turned his men around and ordered them to attack the Muslims from behind. The Muslims were taken completely by surprise. The Quraysh then began attacking from both sides at once. Many Muslims were killed and instead of winning they began to lose the battle.

To add to the confusion, it was rumoured that the Prophet ﷺ had been killed. When the Muslims heard this they were at a loss to know what to do. Then a man named Anas called out, 'Brothers! If Muḥammad ﷺ has been killed what will your lives be worth without him? Don't think about living or dying. Fight for Allah. Get up and die the way Muḥammad ﷺ died!' and on hearing these words the Muslims took courage.

There had been several cavalry attacks on the position held by the Prophet ﷺ and his companions and the Prophet's cheek had been badly gashed. As the Meccans closed in again he called out, 'Who will sell his life for us?' At this, five Anṣār got up and fought until they were killed, one by one. Their places were soon taken, however, by a number of Muslims who drove off the attackers. Amongst the defending Muslims was Abū Dujānah who put his arms around the Prophet ﷺ and made himself into a human shield. Throughout the remainder of the battle he held on to the Prophet ﷺ, but as the fighting drew to a close he suddenly let go. Abū Dujānah was dead, killed by the many arrows in his back that had been aimed at the Prophet ﷺ.

With the defeat of the Muslims, Quraysh were at last avenged. As they left the field of battle Abū Sufyān called out to his men, 'You have done well; victory in war goes by turns—today in exchange for Badr!'

When he heard this, the Prophet ﷺ told 'Umar to answer him, saying, 'Allah is Most High and Most Glorious. We are not equal. Our dead are in Paradise and your dead are in Hell!' The Muslim soldiers then followed the departing Quraysh part of the way to make sure they were not going to attack Medina.

After the enemy had left, the Prophet ﷺ made his way around the battle-field to see the extent of the Muslim losses. Many of the most faithful Muslims had been killed. Among the dead, the Prophet ﷺ found the body of his closest friend and uncle, Ḥamzah, who had been killed by the slave, Waḥshī. At the sight of this, the Prophet ﷺ said, 'There will never be a moment as sad for me as this.' Ḥamzah's sister, Ṣafiyya, came to pray and ask forgiveness for her brother, saying 'We belong to Allah and to Allah we are returning.'

After the Prophet ﷺ had prayed over the many dead, he said, 'I tell you that no one has been wounded in Allah's cause but Allah will remember him and on the Day of Resurrection will raise him from the dead. Look for the one who has learned most of the Koran and put him in front of his companions in the grave.' They were buried where they had fallen as martyrs. Of them Allah says:

In the Name of Allah, the Beneficent, the Merciful
Do not Think that those, who were killed for Allah's sake are dead. Nay, they are alive.

With their Lord they have provision.
Jubilant (are they) because of that which Allah hath
bestowed upon them of His bounty, rejoicing for
the sake of those that have not yet joined them
because they have nothing to fear or grieve over.

(*Koran* iii.169–70)

It is said that the Prophet ﷺ swore that no Muslim who had died for his beliefs would want to come back to life for a single hour, even if he could own the whole world, unless he could return and fight for Allah and be killed a second time.

The Muslims realised that their defeat had been caused by their disobedience to the Prophet ﷺ. The Koran tells us that the Muslims had been tested by Allah at Uhud and had failed but that Allah forgave them their weakness.

In the Name of Allah, the Beneficent, the Merciful

Some of you there are that desire this world,
and some of you there are that desire the next world.
Then He turned you from them, that He might try you;
and He has forgiven you; and Allah is bounteous
to the believers.

(*Koran* iii.145)

People living nowadays should learn from the lessons learned by the early Muslims at Uhud. Disobedience to the Prophet ﷺ and love for the things of this world caused their defeat. The same can happen to us as well. Even if we have no battle like Uhud to fight, we can still die for Allah's sake by fighting what is bad in ourselves.

When the Prophet ﷺ came back from a battle he said to his men, 'We have returned from the lesser war to the greater war.' He meant by this that the struggle that goes on within every human being to become a better person is the more difficult battle.

THE BATTLE OF THE TRENCH

WHEN the Prophet ﷺ first arrived in Medina, the Jews who were living there had welcomed him. The Prophet ﷺ had returned their greeting, as he wished to be on good terms with them. An agreement was also reached between the Muslims and the Jews, which gave the Jews the freedom to practise their religion and which also set out their rights and their duties. Among these duties was that in the case of war with Quraysh, the Jews would fight on the side of the Muslims.

Despite this agreement, however, some of the Jewish tribes, who resented the Prophet's presence in Medina, soon began to cause trouble amongst the Muslims. They tried to set the Muslim Emigrants from Mecca and the Anṣār against each other. The troublemakers were given many warnings but they continued to be a nuisance. In the end, the Muslims had no choice but to drive them from Medina. A new agreement was offered those Jews who remained but the trouble did not end there. One of the Jewish tribes, the Bani Nadir, plotted to murder the Prophet ﷺ but their plan was discovered and they, too, were exiled from the city.

Knowing that they could not defeat the Muslims themselves, some of the leaders of the exiled Jews secretly went to Mecca to enlist the help of Quraysh. Knowing what the Meccans would like to hear, they pretended to believe in the same things. They said that they thought that the old Arab tradition was better than the teachings of the Prophet Muḥammad ﷺ and that they believed that the Quraysh religion of worshipping many idols was better than the Prophet's with only one God. Then the Jews told them that if all the Arab tribes attacked Medina, the Jews inside the city would help to defeat the Prophet ﷺ and Islam once and for all.

The leaders of Quraysh were pleased to hear all this and seizing on what seemed to them a very good opportunity, agreed to the plan and began to gather together a formidable army. In the meantime in Medina, only one Jewish tribe, the Bani Qurayẓah, refused to betray the Muslims.

Eventually the Muslims learned of the preparations being made for war in Mecca and of the plotting of the Jews within Medina itself. The betrayal of the Muslims by the Jews did not surprise the Prophet ﷺ, who said of them: 'The hearts of the Jews have become closed to the truth. They have forgotten what Moses taught them long ago—that there is only one God.'

> *In the Name of Allah, the Beneficent, the Merciful*
> *The likeness of those who are entrusted with the Law of Moses, yet apply it not, is as the likeness of the ass carrying books. Evil is the likeness of the people who deny the revelations of Allah. And Allah guideth not wrongdoing folk.*
>
> (*Koran* lxii.5)

The Muslims wondered how they could defend Medina. They heard that Abū Sufyān was coming to attack them with an enormous army which included many other Arab tribes, as well as Quraysh. What were they to do with only a single week to prepare? The Prophet ﷺ and his men knew that it would be impossible for them to fight off all these tribes! The only thing they could do was to stay inside the city and try to defend it as best they could.

Now among the people of Medina was a Persian named Salmān, who had come to live in the city some time before the Prophet's arrival there. As a convert to Christianity he had travelled to Medina after Christian sages had told him that a Prophet would be born in Arabia. On arriving in Medina he was, however, sold into slavery by the merchants with whom he had travelled. Later he became a Muslim, gained his freedom and became a member of the Prophet's household.

When the people gathered to discuss a plan of action against the approaching enemy, Salmān was present and it was he who suggested that they should dig a trench around the city. The Prophet ﷺ thought this a good idea, so the Muslims set to work, although it was in the middle of winter. They worked day and night, digging the trench as quickly as possible. The Prophet ﷺ himself carried rocks and when the men were tired he gave them the will to carry on. Someone later recalled how beautiful he looked, dressed in a red cloak with dust upon his breast and his dark hair nearly reaching his shoulders.

There was little food at this time and the men were often hungry as they worked. On one occasion, however, a little girl gave some dates to the Prophet ﷺ, which he spread out on a cloth. The men were then called to eat and the dates kept increasing in number until everyone had been fed. Even after everyone had eaten their fill, the dates continued to increase so that there were more than the cloth could hold.

Similarly, there is the story of the lamb, that has come down to us from one who was there:

> 'We worked with the Apostle at the trench. I had a half-grown lamb and I thought it would be a good thing to cook it for Allah's Messenger. I told my wife to grind barley and make some bread for us. I killed the lamb and we roasted it for the Prophet ﷺ. When night fell and he was about to leave the trench, I told him we had prepared bread and meat and invited him to our home. I wanted him to come on his own, but when I said this he sent someone to call all the men to come along. Everyone arrived and the food was served. He blessed it and invoked the Name of Allah over it. Then he ate and so did all the others. As soon as one lot were satisfied, another group came until all the diggers had eaten enough, but still there was food to spare.'

On March 24, 627 A.D., Abū Sufyān arrived with more than ten thousand men. The Muslims numbered only three thousand. Quraysh and their allies surrounded Medina but between the two armies was the long, wide trench. The Prophet ﷺ and his men stayed behind this trench for nearly a month defending the city against their more powerful enemy. Many times enemy warriors tried to cross the trench and enter the city, but each time they were pushed back by the Muslims. The Muslims were afraid that if any did manage to cross over, the Jews inside Medina would join forces with them and the Muslims would be beaten. The Jewish tribe of Bani Qurayẓah, who had stood

by the agreement with the Muslims, were pressed by a Jewish emissary from the enemy without, to break their promise. Eventually they agreed to do so and when the news of this reached the Prophet ﷺ and his Companions they were greatly troubled. Sa'd ibn Mu'ādh, the leader of the tribe of Aws, was sent by the Prophet ﷺ with two other men to find out if this were true. When they arrived in the part of Medina where the Jews lived, they found that things were even worse than they had previously thought. Sa'd ibn Mu'ādh, whose tribe was closely allied with the Bani Qurayẓah, tried to persuade their leader not to break the treaty with the Muslims, but he refused to listen. This meant that the Muslims could not relax their guard for one moment, for they were now threatened not only by the enemy beyond the trench, but by the Bani Qurayẓah, within the walls of the city.

Things became more difficult for the Muslims day by day. It was extremely cold and food began to run out. To make matters worse, the Bani Qurayẓah began openly and actively to join forces with the other Jews and cut off all supplies to the Muslims, including food. The enemies of Islam then planned how to capture Medina.

The situation looked desperate and the Prophet ﷺ prayed to Allah to help the Muslims defeat their enemies. That very night a sandstorm blew up which buried the tents of Quraysh. The storm continued for three days and three nights making it impossible for the enemy to light a fire to cook a meal or warm themselves by.

On one of these dark nights the Prophet ﷺ asked one of his men, Ḥudhayfah ibn al-Yamān, to go on a dangerous mission. The Prophet ﷺ told him to make his way across the trench to the enemy camp where he should find out what they were doing.

With much difficulty Ḥudhayfah crossed the trench and made his way to a circle of Quraysh warriors talking in the darkness. He sat near them, but as there was no fire, no one noticed him. He then heard Abū Sufyān's voice: 'Let us go home!' he said. 'We have had enough. The horses and camels are dying, the tents keep blowing away, most of the equipment has been lost, and we cannot cook our food. There is no reason to stay!'

Shortly after hearing this Ḥudhayfah made his way quickly and quietly back across the trench and the next morning the Muslims rejoiced to find that what he had overheard had come true—Quraysh and their allies had gone away! The siege of Medina had ended in a great victory for Islam.

But this was not to be the end of the difficulties, for the Archangel Gabriel came to the Prophet ﷺ and told him that he should punish the Bani Qurayẓah for betraying him and the Muslims. On hearing this, the Prophet ﷺ ordered the Muslims to march against the Bani Qurayẓah as they hid in their fortress. The Muslims besieged them for twenty-five days until they finally gave in. On surrendering, they asked the Prophet ﷺ to let someone judge their case, and he agreed. He also allowed them to choose who would give the ruling.

The man chosen to judge the Bani Qurayẓah was Sa'd ibn Mu'ādh, leader of the Aws, a tribe which had always protected the Qurayẓah in the past. Sa'd ibn Mu'ādh, who had himself been wounded in the battle, decided that the Jews should be tried by their own Holy Law, according to which anyone who broke a treaty would be put to death. As a result all the men of the Bani Qurayẓah were executed and the women and children made captive.

If the Jews had succeeded in their pact, Islam would have been destroyed. Instead, from that day on, Medina became a city where only Muslims lived.

Very soon after peace had been restored to Medina, Sa'd ibn Mu'ādh died of his wounds. It was said that the Archangel Gabriel came in the middle of that night and said to the Prophet ﷺ 'O Muḥammad, who is this dead man? When he arrived, the doors of heaven opened and the Throne of Allah shook.'

The Prophet ﷺ got up as soon as he heard this, but found that Sa'd was already dead. Although he had been a heavy man, the men who carried his body to the grave found it quite light. They were told that the angels were helping them. When he was buried, the Prophet ﷺ said three times, 'Subḥān Allah!' (Glory be to Allah!), and 'Allāhu Akbar!' (Allah is Most Great!) When asked why he did this, he replied, 'The grave was tight for this good man, until Allah eased it for him.' This is one of the rewards that Allah gives to martyrs and good Muslims.

THE TREATY OF ḤUDAYBIYAH

QURAYSH had tried to destroy Islam but had failed. The number of Muslims grew and their armies increased from three hundred at the battle of Badr, seven hundred at the battle of 'Uhud, to three thousand at the battle of the Trench.

After the annual fast of Ramadan, the Prophet ﷺ had a dream which indicated that the Muslims should go to Mecca for the pilgrimage. One thousand and four hundred Muslims got ready to go with him on the Lesser Pilgrimage called 'the *'Umra*'. They dressed in white and went unarmed to show Quraysh that they had come to make the pilgrimage and not to fight. When Quraysh heard that the Prophet ﷺ was on his way, they sent troops with Khālid ibn al-Walīd to stop the Muslims from entering the city.

To avoid meeting this small army the Prophet ﷺ changed his route and led the men through rugged mountain passes. When they reached easier ground he told them, 'Say, we ask Allah's forgiveness and we repent towards Him.' At Ḥudaybiyah, south of Mecca, the Prophet's camel knelt down and refused to go any further. The Muslims thought she was either stubborn or tired, but the Prophet ﷺ said: 'The same power that once stopped the elephant from entering Mecca is now stopping us!' He then ordered them to make camp, which they did, although they all hoped they would travel on to the sacred Ka'bah the following day.

On setting up camp, the believers were dismayed to find that the springs were almost dry. When he heard this the Messenger of Allah ﷺ instructed a man called Nājiyah to take the bowl of water in which he had performed his ablutions, pour it into the hollows where the small amount of spring water lay, and stir it with his arrows. Nājiyah did as he was told and the fresh water gushed up so suddenly that he was hardly able to get out of the way in time.

Messengers were sent to Quraysh to tell them that the Muslims had come only for the pilgrimage, to worship Allah at the Holy Ka'bah, and that they wanted to enter the city peacefully. But Quraysh took no notice. Finally, the Prophet's son-in-law, 'Uthmān ibn 'Affān, a wise and respected man, was chosen to go, and the Muslims settled down to wait and see what news he would bring back. After they had waited a long time, the Muslims became very worried. At last they decided that he must have been killed. A state similar to that of Revelation then came upon the Prophet ﷺ. He gathered the Muslims around him under an acacia tree and asked them to swear their allegiance to him, which they did. This pact, which is mentioned in the Koran, became known as the Treaty of Radwan (which means Paradise). Shortly after, 'Uthmān ibn 'Affān returned and the Muslims were relieved to see that no harm had come to him.

Some Meccan warriors tried to attack the Muslim camp but were captured and brought before the Prophet ﷺ, who forgave them when they promised to stop attacking the Muslims. Soon after this, official messengers came from Quraysh and talks began for a peaceful settlement. A man called Suhayl ibn 'Amr was sent by the Meccans to work out a treaty. When the Prophet ﷺ asked 'Alī to write 'In the Name of Allah, the Most Gracious, the Most Merciful', on the top of the page, Suhayl objected, saying 'Write only: bismik Allahumma (in Thy name, O Allah). I don't know him as al-Rahman (the Most Gracious), al-Rahim (the most Merciful).'

The Prophet ﷺ agreed and dictated: 'This is a treaty between Muḥammad the Messenger of Allah and Suhayl ibn 'Amr.'

'Stop!' cried Suhayl, 'I don't believe that you are Rasulallah (the Messenger of Allah). If I thought you were Allah's Messenger, I wouldn't be fighting against you, would I?'

Calmly, the Prophet ﷺ agreed that he should be referred to in the treaty as Muḥammad', son of 'Abd Allāh. The Muslims were very upset at this, and 'Umar furiously cried out, 'Are you not Allah's Messenger, and are we not Muslims? How can we accept such treatment when we are right and they are wrong? This will make people laugh at our religion!'

But the Prophet ﷺ knew what was best and the Treaty of Ḥudaybiyah was signed.

In this treaty the two sides agreed to stop fighting for a period of ten years. It was also agreed that the Muslims should go back to Medina immediately but that they could return the following year for the pilgrimage. This pilgrimage would last three days. In addition, the treaty allowed Muslims wishing to leave Islam and return to Mecca to do so. It also permitted Meccans to leave and become Muslims provided they had the permission of their guardians. The Muslims agreed to send any Meccan who did not have their guardian's permission back to Mecca.

Suhayl's son had come with his father with the idea of joining the Prophet ﷺ but when the treaty was signed he was, of course, forced to return to Mecca. He cried bitterly. The Prophet ﷺ said, 'O Abū Jandal, be patient and control yourself. Allah will provide relief and find a way out for you and others like you.'

The majority of the Muslims were very disappointed when they heard the terms of the agreement and thought that it should not have been accepted. They did not realise that this was in fact a great victory for the Prophet ﷺ, which Allah would later confirm in a Revelation. The agreement made sure that the following year they would enter Mecca peacefully, and in time would result in Muslims becoming stronger and more respected throughout Arabia. At the time the treaty was signed the Muslims could not have foreseen that the number of people who would travel to Medina to become Muslims in the following year would be greater than in all the years before.

Before the Muslims departed, they followed the Prophet's example of making sacrifice and either shaving or cutting their hair. Even though they were unable to visit the sacred mosque, their pilgrimage was accepted by Allah because it had been their true intention.

On the return journey to Medina, the 'Victory' chapter of the Koran was revealed to the Prophet ﷺ. It begins:

In the Name of Allah, the Beneficent, the Merciful

Surely We have given thee (O Muḥammad) a clear victory,
That Allah may forgive thee of thy sin
That which is past and that which is to come,
And may complete His blessings upon thee,
And may guide thee on the right path,
And that Allah may help thee with mighty help. (*Koran* xlviii. 1–3)

Now most of those who left Mecca to join the Prophet ﷺ without the consent of their guardians and were turned back by him as agreed, did not in fact return to Mecca, but lived instead in groups along the seashore. There they were joined by others who had left Mecca but these groups began to endanger Quraysh caravans which were passing by and disrupted their trade. Because of this, Quraysh told the Prophet ﷺ that if he wanted to take these new Muslims, they would not ask for them to be returned. The young men, therefore, joined the Prophet ﷺ and the people in Mecca and Medina grew more at ease with one another. The young men from the seashore were shortly followed by those Muslims who were still living in Abyssinia, and soon the numbers of believers in Medina had doubled.

About this time, Khālid ibn al-Walīd, the great warrior who had defeated the Muslims at Uhud, set out from Mecca for Medina. Along the way he met 'Amr ibn al-'Ās, the clever speaker who had pursued the Muslims when they fled to Abyssinia. 'Amr, who had attempted to find asylum in Abyssinia, had just returned from that country, the Negus having urged him to enter Islam. He asked Khālid, 'Where are you going?' Khālid replied, 'The way has become clear. The man is certainly a Prophet, and by Allah, I am going to become a Muslim. How much longer should I delay?' 'Amr ibn al-'Ās answered, 'I am travelling for the same reason.'

So they both travelled on to Medina to join the Prophet ﷺ.

The two men were, however, worried about meeting the Prophet ﷺ because of having fought against the Muslims in the past. Therefore, when 'Amr came before Allah's Messenger he said, 'O Prophet, will my past faults be forgiven and no mention made of what has gone before?'

The Prophet ﷺ replied, ''Amr, Islam wipes away everything that happened before, as does the *hijrah*.'

A year after the signing of the Treaty of Ḥudaybiyah, the Prophet ﷺ was able to lead two thousand pilgrims on the *'Umra*. Quraysh vacated Mecca and watched the rites from the hills above the city. The agreed period of three days was observed, after which the Muslims returned to Medina.

THE INVITATION

THE peace which the Treaty of Ḥudaybiyah guaranteed for ten years meant that people could travel from all over Arabia to visit the Prophet ﷺ and a great many came to declare their Islam. Also, during this period the Prophet ﷺ decided that the time had come for his message to be taken to other countries, so he sent trusted companions with letters, telling of his message, to

the leaders of the most powerful nations of the day. It is recorded that he said, 'Allah has sent me as a mercy to all men, so take the message from me that Allah has mercy on you.' It is also recorded that some time before, when the Prophet ﷺ was digging before the Battle of the Trench, three flashes of lightning had blazed forth from a rock he had been striving to remove. These flashes had shown him the fortresses of the civilizations to the South, East, and West which were soon to come into Islam.

Now at the time the Prophet ﷺ sent out his message, Abū Sufyān and some other members of Quraysh were trading in Syria, a province of the Eastern Roman Empire (later to be called Byzantium). Also, at about this time the Emperor Heraclius, ruler of this Empire, had a dream, and sadly told visitors to his court in Syria: 'I saw our Empire fall and victory go to a people who do not follow our religion.' At first he thought this must refer to the Jews, and he even had it in mind to kill all the Jews living under his rule. But then an envoy from the governor of Basra arrived with a message for the Emperor: 'O Emperor Heraclius, there are some Arabs in the city who are speaking of wonderful happenings in their country', and he then told of what he had heard about the Prophet ﷺ.

On hearing this Heraclius commanded his soldiers: 'Go and find me someone who can tell me more about this.'

The soldiers, however, did not find those who had been talking about the Prophet ﷺ, but instead found Abū Sufyān and some of his companions and brought them before the Emperor. Heraclius asked, 'Is there anyone among you who is a close relative of the Prophet Muḥammad ﷺ?'

Abū Sufyān replied, 'I am.'

So the Emperor addressed all the questions to him, thinking he would know the Prophet ﷺ best. He said, 'Tell me what is the Prophet's position in your tribe?'

Abū Sufyān said, 'He is a member of our most respected family.'

'Did anyone before him say the kinds of things he says?' the Emperor went on.

'No', was the reply.

'And was he ever accused of lying or cheating?'

'Never.'

And then the Emperor asked: 'And what about his ideas and opinions, and his powers of reasoning?'

'No one has ever had cause to doubt him or find fault with his reasoning', replied Abū Sufyān.

'Who follows him, the proud or the humble?'

'The humble.'

'Do his followers increase or decrease?'

'They increase', said Abū Sufyān, 'none of his followers leave him.'

The Emperor then turned to other matters and asked: 'If he makes a treaty, does he keep it?'

'Yes', Abū Sufyān replied.

'Did you ever fight against him?' enquired the Emperor.

To which Abū Sufyān answered: 'Yes. Sometimes we won, sometimes he won, but he never broke his word in any agreement.'

The Emperor then asked: 'What does he say people must do?'

'To worship one God', said Abū Sufyān. 'He forbids people to worship as their fathers worshipped, and says they must pray to Allah alone, give alms, keep their word, and fulfil their duties and responsibilities.'

Abū Sufyān had spoken the truth even though he was an enemy of the Prophet ﷺ, and did not become a Muslim until the very end of his life. But he was afraid to lie before the members of his caravan who were also there with him. The meeting ended with these words from the Emperor: 'I see from this that he is indeed a Prophet. You said that his followers do not leave him which proves they have true faith, for faith does not enter the heart and then go away. I knew he was coming and if what you say is true, he will surely conquer me. If I were with him now, I would wash his feet. You may leave now.'

It was not long after this that the messenger, Diḥyah, arrived at the Syrian court bearing the Prophet Muḥammad's letter which said, 'If you accept Islam you will be safe, and Allah will give you a double reward. If you do not, you will have to live with the results of your decision.'

Heraclius grabbed the letter. He was so upset he could hardly control himself. He said to Diḥyah, 'I know your master is a true Prophet of Allah. Our books tell of his coming. If I were not afraid that the Romans would kill me, I would join Islam. You must visit Bishop Ḍaghāṭir and tell him everything. His word is more respected among the people than mine.'

So Diḥyah related the message to the Bishop and when he heard it, Ḍaghāṭir said, 'Yes, your master, whom we call Aḥmad, is mentioned in our scriptures.' He then changed from his black robes into white ones and went and spoke to the people gathered in the church. 'O Romans, a letter has come to us from Aḥmad, in which he calls us to Allah. I bear witness that there is no divinity but Allah and that Aḥmad is his slave and messenger.' (Aḥmad is another name for the Prophet Muḥammad.) But on hearing this the crowd grew angry and attacked Ḍaghāṭir, beating him until he was dead.

Heraclius was afraid that the same thing would happen to him, so he spoke to his generals from a balcony saying, 'O Romans! A man has written to me calling me to his religion. I believe he is truly the Prophet we have been told to expect. Let us follow him so that we can be happy in this world and the next.' The Romans cried out in anger when they heard this, so Heraclius quickly said, 'I was only pretending; I wanted to see how strong your faith was. I am pleased to see that you are true to your religion.' Heraclius then suggested that they pay a tax or give land to the Muslims in order to maintain peace, but the Romans refused. Realizing that he could do no more, and knowing that one day Islam would conquer Syria, Heraclius left the province and returned to Constantinople, the capital of the Eastern Roman Empire. As he rode away he turned around to look back and said, 'Goodbye for the last time, O land of Syria!'

Meanwhile, another of the Prophet's messengers arrived at the palace of Chosroes, the Shah (or King) of Persia, where he was told by the royal guard: 'When you see the Shah, you must bow and not lift your head until he speaks to you.'

To this the Prophet's messenger replied, 'I will never do that. I bow only to Allah.' 'Then the Shah will not accept the letter you bring', they said.

And when the time came for the messenger to see him, the Shah was indeed very surprised to see the man holding his head high and refusing to kneel respectfully before him like everyone else. Nonetheless, the Shah still read out the letter:

In the Name of Allah, the Beneficent, the Most Merciful

> from Muḥammad, Messenger of Allah to Chosroes, Shah of Persia.
>
> Peace be upon those who follow the truth, who believe in Allah and His Prophet and who testify that there is no divinity but Allah and that Muḥammad is His Messenger. I ask you in the Name of Allah, because I am His Messenger, to warn your people that if they do not accept His Message, they must live with the consequences. Become Muslim and you will be safe. If you refuse to tell them you will be to blame for the ignorance of your subjects.

The Shah was furious when he read this and tore the letter into little pieces.

When the messenger returned to Arabia and told the Prophet ﷺ what Chosroes had done, the Prophet ﷺ said, 'May Allah also tear his kingdom into little pieces.' And several years later it happened just as the Prophet ﷺ had said it would.

As with Syria and Persia, a messenger was also sent to the Negus (or King) of Abyssinia, with the following letter:

> Peace. Praise be to Allah, the King, the All-Holy, the Peacemaker, the Keeper of Faith, the Watcher.
>
> *He is Allah, there is no divinity but He,*
> *the Sovereign Lord, the Holy One, the All-peaceable,*
> *the Keeper of Faith, the Guardian, the Majestic,*
> *the Compeller, the All-sublime. Glorified be Allah*
> *from all that they associate with Him.*
>
> (*Koran* lix.23)
>
> And I testify that Jesus, son of Mary, is the spirit of Allah and His Word which He cast to Mary the Virgin, the good, the pure, so that she conceived Jesus. Allah Created him from His Spirit and His Breath as He created Adam by His Hand and His Breath. I call you to Allah, the Unique, without partner, to His obedience, and to follow me and to believe in that which came to me, for I am the Messenger of Allah. Peace be upon all those who follow true guidance.

The King of Abyssinia was a very wise man, and was thought by the world to be a good Christian. He had, of course, already heard of the Prophet ﷺ and his religion from the Muslims who had sought refuge in his country years before. He was deeply moved by the letter and when he came down from his throne it was not just to show his respect but also to declare that he was already a Muslim.

He answered the Prophet's letter with one of his own.

> To Muḥammad the Prophet of Allah from the Negus al-Asham, King of Abyssinia.
>
> Assalamu aleikum O Prophet of Allah wa rahmatullah wa barakatuhu
>
> There is none like Him who has guided me to Islam.
>
> I received your letter, O Messenger of Allah. Some of your followers, as well as your cousin Ja'far, still live here. I believe you are truly the Messenger of God and reaffirm the pledge of allegiance I made to you some time ago before your cousin Ja'far, at whose hand I joined Islam and surrendered to the Lord of the Worlds.

A fourth messenger had, in the meantime, travelled by boat to Alexandria to meet the Muqawqis, the ruler of Egypt, who was a Coptic Christian. In his letter, the Prophet ﷺ invited the Muqawqis to accept Islam, because a Christian who believed in the message of Jesus should also believe in him, for he had come with the same message from Allah.

It read:

> *In the Name of Allah, the Beneficent, the Most Merciful,*
> from Muḥammad, son of 'Abd Allāh to the great Copt.
>
> Peace be upon whoever follows the Truth. I beseech you to accept Islam. Become a Muslim. Allah will reward you twice. If you refuse, you will carry the blame for not allowing your people to share in this blessing.

The Muqawqis showed respect for what the letter said. He treated the messenger well, and sent many presents with him for the Prophet ﷺ, but he did not become a Muslim.

Although only Abyssinia responded to the Prophet's call to Islam, all was not lost, for a few years later Persia, Syria and Egypt all became Muslim countries.

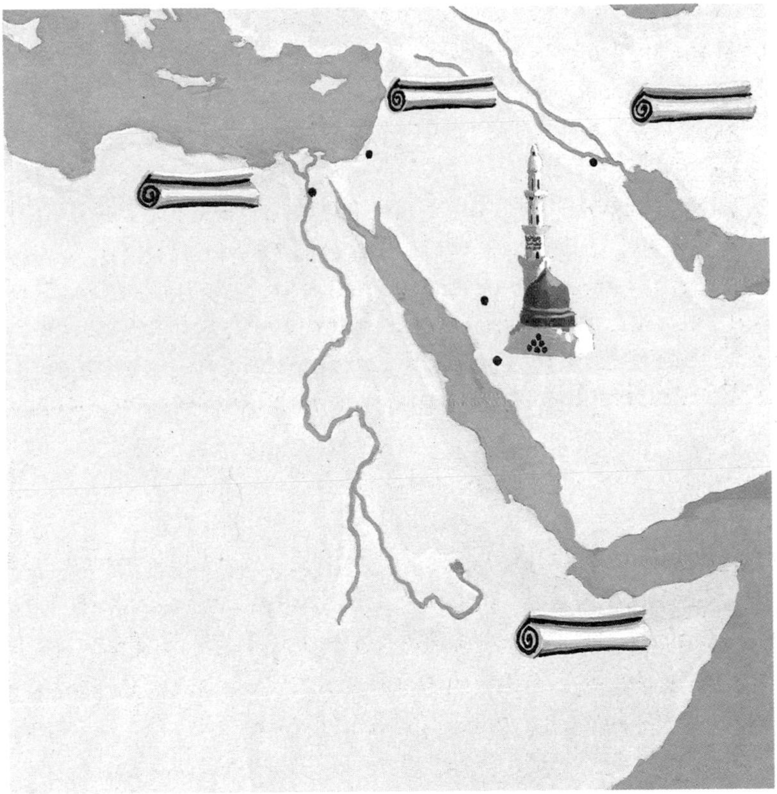

THE ENTRY INTO MECCA

DESPITE the improved relations between Mecca and Medina after the signing of the Treaty of Ḥudaybiyah, the ten-year peace was to be broken by Quraysh who, with their allies, the Bani Bakr, attacked the Khuzāʿah tribe. Now Khuzāʿah were allies of the Muslims and when the Prophet ﷺ heard of the attack he immediately ordered his men to prepare for war. When they were ready he told them that their destination was Mecca and, as he did not want any fighting within the walls of the city, he told them they must move quickly and take the enemy by surprise. In this way the Meccans would not have time to prepare for war and, being surrounded would have to surrender. The Muslims would then be able to take the city without injury or loss of life to anyone.

When the Muslim army, which numbered ten thousand, set out for Mecca, it was the month of Ramadan in the eighth year of the *Hijrah*. Many of the men kept the fast, even though they were not obliged to because they were travelling. Everyone was jubilant because they were going to Mecca, especially as some of them had not seen their homes in the city for eight long years.

In the meantime, the Prophet's uncle, al-ʿAbbās, had decided that the time had come for him and his wife to leave Mecca and join the Prophet ﷺ in Medina. They did not, however, have to go far as after a distance of only twenty-five kilometres they came across the Muslim camp. When the Prophet ﷺ saw them he said, 'Uncle, your emigration is the last emigration. My prophecy is the last prophecy.' Al-ʿAbbās then joined the army and his wife went on to the safety of Medina.

Night fell and the Muslims made fires to light their camp. The Meccans, looking out of the city, were amazed to see the many fires, and Abū Sufyān went all over Mecca trying to find out whose camp it was. Suddenly he saw al-ʿAbbās riding towards him from the direction of the fires. He was returning as a messenger of peace from the Prophet ﷺ and said to Abū Sufyān, 'The Muslims have come with a large army. They do not wish to fight, only to enter the city. It would be better to surrender and not fight. Come under my protection and meet the Prophet ﷺ.'

Abū Sufyān agreed, and got up behind al-ʿAbbās, who was riding the Prophet's white mule. It was still night as they entered the Muslim camp. Each time they passed a fire, someone would call out, 'Who goes there?' None of them recognized the stranger as the leader of their enemy but all knew al-ʿAbbās and so let them through.

As they passed by ʿUmar, however, he immediately recognized Abū Sufyān and yelled out, 'Abū Sufyān! The enemy of Allah!' He ran after them intending to kill his enemy but al-ʿAbbās made the mule go faster. They reached the Prophet's tent just before ʿUmar, who rushed in after them quite out of breath. ʿUmar begged the Prophet ﷺ, 'O Messenger of Allah, let me end the life of Abū Sufyān, this enemy of Islam, who has led the Quraysh armies in their attacks on us!'

Al-ʿAbbās interrupted, saying, 'I have sworn to protect him during his time here', whereupon the Prophet ﷺ told his uncle to take Abū Sufyān to his tent for the night.

In the morning Abū Sufyān was taken to the Prophet ﷺ who said, 'Abū Sufyān! Have you not yet realized that there is no divinity but Allah?'

To this Abū Sufyān replied, 'If there had been another he surely would have helped me by now.'

'Shame on you, Abū Sufyān', responded the Prophet ﷺ, 'it is time you realized that I am truly Allah's Messenger.'

After a moment or two, Abū Sufyān, who remembered how ʿUmar had not been allowed to kill him, replied: 'I can see you are a generous and forgiving man but I still cannot be sure of that.'

At this, al-ʿAbbās, who had been standing nearby turned to him and said: 'Believe, as I do now.'

Abū Sufyān stood quietly for a moment, then in a calm, clear voice swore in front of everyone, 'There is no divinity but Allah, and Muḥammad is the Messenger of Allah.'

The Prophet ﷺ then told Abū Sufyān to go back to Mecca and tell the people that the Muslims would enter the city the next morning. Before he left, however, al-'Abbās suggested to the Prophet ﷺ that as Abū Sufyān was a proud man, it would be good to give him an honourable position. The Prophet ﷺ took this advice, saying to Abū Sufyān, 'Tell the people that when we enter, anyone seeking refuge in your house will be safe.' This was a great honour for Abū Sufyān. In addition, the Prophet ﷺ told him to assure the Meccans that those who remained in their own homes or at the Ka'bah would also be protected.

Abū Sufyān returned quickly to the city. He made straight for the hill Hagar had climbed in her search for water and from which the Prophet ﷺ later spoke, and called upon Quraysh to come to him. Abū Sufyān then spoke to the people, 'O people of Mecca, the fires we saw all around us were the camp fires of Muḥammad and his men. He has come with a strong army and there are too many for us to fight. It is best, therefore, to surrender. Anyone who stays in my house, or in his own home, or at the Ka'bah will be safe.'

Early next day, the Muslims entered Mecca from all sides. They had been ordered to cause no harm unless anyone tried to stop them entering. When the Prophet ﷺ arrived, he got off his camel, bowed down on the ground and thanked Allah for this victory. When the unbelievers saw this, they knew that the Prophet ﷺ had come in peace. People began leaving their homes and running towards the Ka'bah. When they arrived there, they found the Prophet ﷺ performing the ritual encircling of the Ka'bah, the *tawaf*, on his camel, surrounded by the Muslims. When he had finished, he said, 'There is no divinity except Allah and He has no partner. Men and women of Quraysh, be not proud for all are equal; we are all the sons of Adam, and Adam was made of dust.' Then he recited this verse to them:

> *In the Name of Allah, the Beneficent, the Merciful*
> *O mankind! Lo! We have created you male and*
> *female, and have made you nations and tribes so*
> *you may know each another. Surely the noblest of you,*
> *in the sight of Allah, is the best in conduct.*
> *Lo! Allah is All-knowing, All-aware.*

(*Koran* xlix.13)

After this he said to them: 'O Quraysh, what do you think I am going to do to you?'

The people thought carefully before answering because they knew that according to the laws of war they could all be taken prisoner. They also knew, however, that the Prophet Muḥammad ﷺ was generous, so they replied, 'You will treat us as a kind nephew and a generous brother would.'

To this he replied with the words used by the Prophet Joseph when his brothers came to Egypt: 'God forgives you and He is the Most Merciful of the Merciful.' Later the Prophet ﷺ went to the hill of Ṣafā and there the crowd followed him and surged forward, taking his hand one by one, to declare themselves Muslim.

He then turned to the Ka'bah and, pointing his staff at the three hundred and sixty-five idols which were placed there, recited from the Koran:

In the Name of Allah, the Beneficent, the Merciful
. . . Truth has come and falsehood has vanished away.
Lo! Falsehood is ever bound to vanish.

(*Koran* xvii.81)

At this, each idol fell over onto its face. Together with his followers the Prophet ﷺ then proceeded to purify the Ka'bah, after which he ordered Bilāl to climb on top of it and perform the call to prayer. Since then the call to prayer has been heard five times a day in Mecca. The Ka'bah, the House of Allah, has served the purpose for which it was built by Abraham thousands of years ago, as a sanctuary for the worship of Allah, our Creator, and Mecca continues to be the spiritual centre of Islam.

On the day Mecca was conquered, the Prophet ﷺ addressed the people, saying:

> 'Allah made Mecca holy the day He created heaven and earth and it is the Holy of Holies until the Resurrection Day. It is not lawful for anyone who believes in Allah and the Last Day to shed blood therein, nor to cut down trees therein. It was not lawful for anyone before me and it will not be lawful for anyone after me. Indeed it is not lawful for me except at this time, only Allah's anger against his people makes it permissible. Mecca has now regained its former holiness. Let those here now go forth and tell others.'

THE LESSON OF PRIDE AT THE VALLEY OF ḤUNAYN

ISLAM flourished in Mecca and the Muslims became stronger and stronger. But south of Mecca lived a tribe of warriors called Hawāzin, who had not become Muslim. They made an agreement with another tribe from Ṭā'if, called Thaqīf, to fight the Muslims and destroy them before they could spread their religion throughout Arabia.

The Thaqīf, who were known for their courage, soon won the support of other tribes living around the Ṭā'if area, especially when such tribes were told: 'Look what has happened! If Quraysh, the largest tribe of all, have fallen to Muḥammad, it is only a matter of time before the same will happen to the rest of us. We should strike now before the Muslims are established in Mecca and have the support of Quraysh.'

The Chief of one of these tribes, a fearless warrior called Mālik ibn 'Awf, was chosen as the leader. He put forward a plan: 'You should all go out to battle accompanied by your families, your tents, your sheep and goats, for with all your belongings at stake, none of you will dare give up the fight.'

Everyone agreed with Mālik except an old, blind man called Dorayd. He had been a great warrior in his day and because of his experience and valuable advice, still accompanied the men into battle. 'I don't like Mālik's plan', he insisted. 'If a man is so cowardly as to leave a battle, then he will leave his family as well. The women and children will be a great worry to us and if we are defeated all our wealth will fall into enemy hands.' But Mālik ignored this advice and stuck to his original plan.

When the Prophet ﷺ heard what the enemy tribes were planning, he found himself forced to fight and ordered his army towards Ṭā'if. He had twelve thousand men and the enemy only four thousand. The Muslims were proud of their strength and as they looked around at their number, said to themselves, 'We will never be defeated!' On hearing this the Prophet ﷺ knew that the Muslims had become too proud and because of this would not succeed. He warned them, 'Look to Allah and not to your own strength.'

The time for battle came. The Muslim army advanced along the Ḥunayn path, a narrow way in the rugged mountains, towards the valley where the Hawāzin and the other tribes were waiting. It was very early morning and not yet light. The Muslims were unaware that, under cover of darkness, the Hawāzin warriors had already climbed up the mountain and were waiting for them. As soon as all the Muslims were trapped in the narrow passage-way below, the Hawāzin ambushed them. First they threw rocks down upon them and then attacked with arrows and swords.

In surprise and fear, the Muslims started to retreat. The Prophet ﷺ was bitterly disappointed to see them fleeing in terror but he stayed firmly in his place with Abū Bakr, 'Alī, his uncle al-'Abbās, and a few companions at his side. Al-'Abbās then called to the Muslims to return and not to abandon the Prophet ﷺ. Ashamed at what they had done, and seeing the Prophet ﷺ facing the enemy almost alone, the Muslims quickly returned to fight. Then Allah sent His angels—*the hosts ye cannot see*—to their aid. A fierce battle followed. The Muslim warriors advanced, attacking furiously, driving the Hawāzin back from the path into the valley, where the fighting went on long and hard. At the end of the day the Muslims won but not before having learnt a hard lesson about the danger of pride.

Just as the old man had predicted, the defeated enemy fled, leaving their families and possessions to be captured. Later all the leaders of the tribes except one came to ask for them back and to declare their acceptance of Islam. The Prophet ﷺ forgave them and returned their families to them, but not their belongings.

The one exception was the leader of Hawāzin. He fled to Ṭā'if, where he sought protection in the castle, but the Muslims pursued him and surrounded the city, which they besieged for about three weeks. They tried to break into the castle but after losing many men in the attempt the Prophet ﷺ ordered a withdrawal. The story did not end there, however, for shortly afterwards Hawāzin and most of the other tribes came to Mecca and declared themselves Muslim, including Mālik ibn 'Awf, who had led them in battle and whom the Prophet ﷺ now made their leader.

After the battle of the Ḥunayn Valley, the Prophet ﷺ distributed what goods had been taken between the people of Quraysh and the other Bedouin tribes. The Anṣār from Medina, who had been his only support during the long hard years before the conquest of Mecca, received nothing. They felt angry about this and went to the Prophet ﷺ to complain. He said to them, 'What is this I hear of you? Do you think badly of me? Did I not come to you when you did not know the truth and Allah guided you; when you were poor and Allah made you rich; when you were enemies and Allah softened your hearts? Are you covetous for the things of this world that I must use to gain people's trust so that I can then lead them to Islam? Surely for you Islam is enough? Are you not satisfied that while some men take away flocks and herds you take Allah's Messenger back with you to Medina?'

On hearing this, all the men felt very contrite and began to weep. Then with great humility and reverence their spokesman said: 'We are indeed well pleased to have Allah's Messenger as our gift in this life.'

Perhaps we could ask ourselves the same question. Are we not blessed to have the Prophet Muḥammad ﷺ and the Book, guiding us in what really matters for ever and ever? Is this not so much more important than thinking about the momentary pleasures of the day?

Shortly after this the Anṣār left for Medina accompanied by the Prophet ﷺ. He could have stayed among his own people and lived out his days in Mecca, but he returned as he had promised, to live among the people of Medina, which was a great blessing for them.

In the Name of Allah, the Beneficent, the Merciful

Allah gave you victory on many fields and on the
day of Ḥunayn, when you exulted in your great numbers it
was of no help to you, and the earth, vast as it is, was
straitened for you; then you turned back in flight;
Then Allah sent His peace of reassurance down upon
His Messenger and upon the believers, and sent down
hosts you could not see, and punished those who did not believe.
Such is the reward of disbelievers.
Then afterwards Allah will relent toward whom He
will; for Allah is Forgiving, Merciful. (*Koran* ix.25–27)

TABUK—THE TEST OF FAITH

NEWS of the growing power of the Muslims, as more and more of Arabia followed the Prophet ﷺ, eventually reached Heraclius, Emperor of the Eastern Roman Empire. The Romans saw the uniting of the Arabs in Islam as a possible threat to their Empire and the Emperor's advisors and generals, therefore, decided that the best thing to do would be to attack the Muslims from the north and east at the same time and destroy Islam once and for all. Two years had passed since Heraclius had told them of the Prophet's letter asking them to submit to Islam, but just as then, they were in no mood now to listen to such ideas.

When the Prophet ﷺ heard of the Romans' plans, he decided that it would be better to meet the Roman army in Tabūk, some 500 kilometres from Medina on the route to Syria, than to await an attack on Medina. One reason for this decision was that the Prophet ﷺ felt that if the Muslims were defeated at Medina, the city as well as the army would be taken, which would mean the end of Islam. This was a very hard decision for him to make because not only was Tabūk a very long way away, but it was also harvest time and a particularly hot year. Added to this was the fact that the enemy had an enormous army.

Now at this time there were some people living in Medina who were not true believers. They were called 'hypocrites' because they pretended to believe but hid what was truly in their hearts. When the Prophet ﷺ called everyone to war, these hypocrites tried to create fear and doubt among the Muslims, saying 'How can we hope to defeat the Romans whose great empire stretches over vast areas of the world? And even if we could, we will not get the chance because the long journey and the heat will defeat us first. In any case, our crops and fruits are ready to be harvested; how can we leave them? We will be ruined if we do!'

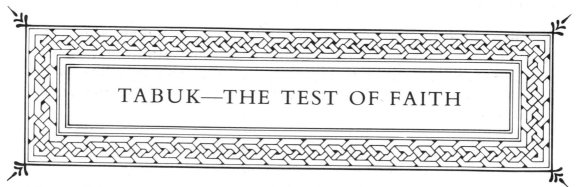

All that the hypocrites said severely tested the Muslims. Who would continue to fight for his religion against such odds? Who would have the courage to give his wealth to help equip an army? This test of faith would indeed show who the true Muslims were. On this question, Allah revealed the following verse:

> *In the Name of Allah, the Beneficent, the Merciful*
>
> *O you who believe! What aileth you that when it*
> *is said unto you: Go forth in the way of Allah,*
> *you are bowed down to the ground with heaviness.*
> *Do you take pleasure in the life of the world*
> *rather than in the Hereafter? The comfort of the*
> *life of the world is but little in the Hereafter.* (*Koran* ix.38)

To form and equip an army the Prophet ﷺ needed a great deal of money and despite all that the hypocrites had said, many Muslims, especially the Prophet's close friends, were willing to help. ʿUthmān ibn ʿAffān, for instance, generously provided horses and arms for ten thousand soldiers and Abū Bakr gave all that he had in the world. ʿUmar, too, gave a great deal, and in this way the Prophet ﷺ was able to equip an army of forty thousand soldiers.

Finally everything was ready but just as they were about to leave, seven more men came to the Prophet ﷺ to ask if they could go with him. Unfortunately, he had to refuse because there were no animals for them to ride. The seven men were so upset that they wept as they left. With nothing more to be done, the army moved off, but just then several spare camels were found. On learning of this, the Prophet ﷺ sent for the seven men, who were overjoyed to find that they could join him in his fight.

By now the Romans had heard that the Muslims were coming out to meet them. They felt even more sure of victory when they heard this because they believed that it would be quite impossible for an army to cross a waterless desert in the scorching summer sun. Even if by some miracle the Muslims succeeded, they would be so exhausted that it would be easy to defeat them.

As it happened, the heat was so intense and the journey so difficult that several Muslims did turn back. The Prophet ﷺ and most of the others,

however, continued until they finally ran out of water. The expedition now seemed hopeless as the men grew thirstier and thirstier. The Prophet ﷺ prayed to Allah for help and, as he finished his prayer, the first drops of rain came splashing down. The rain continued to fall until all the Muslims had drunk their fill. That night they slept soundly for the first time in days, refreshed by the water and confident that Bilāl would wake them as usual for the dawn prayer. But Bilāl slept so deeply that he did not wake up. It was the first time that the Muslims had missed a prayer and they were very upset. The Prophet ﷺ, however, was not angry with Bilāl and told the Muslims that they need not be upset because they had not intentionally missed the prayer.

The Prophet ﷺ and his army continued their trek across the desert and finally arrived at the oasis of Tabūk. When they got there, however, they were surprised to find that the Roman army had retreated in fear on hearing of the miraculous crossing of the desert by the Muslims. The Prophet ﷺ waited at the oasis for a while but when it became apparent that the Romans were not going to fight, he gave the order to return home. The enemy was not pursued because the Prophet ﷺ only fought when attacked.

The long march to Tabūk had been yet another test of faith for the Muslims. Even so, there were still some among those who made that heroic journey who were hypocrites, pretending to be sincere while being enemies of Islam in their hearts. No one could have suspected that anyone who had made that journey across the desert with the Prophet ﷺ would be an enemy of his. Realizing this, several hypocrites plotted to kill the Prophet ﷺ by pushing him off the top of a high, rocky passage that ran between the mountains at ʿAqabah.

Before the army reached this rocky passage, however, Allah warned the Prophet ﷺ about this wicked plan. The Prophet ﷺ, therefore, ordered the entire army to travel through the valley while he and his two guards went by way of the cliff. As the plotters approached, he shouted to them so that they could see that he knew of their plan, whereupon they quickly ran back to the army and tried to hide among the rest of the soldiers.

Later, the Prophet ﷺ gathered his followers around him and told them what had happened. He picked out the men who had plotted against him and even told them the exact words they had spoken to each other. Some of the

Prophet's companions said that these men should be killed, but the Prophet ﷺ forgave them.

As soon as he arrived back in Medina, the Prophet ﷺ went to to the mosque and prayed. Many of the hypocrites and the lukewarm who had not gone with him to Tabūk came to give their reasons for not having done so. Three men of spiritual value who had not joined the army were subjected by the Prophet ﷺ to the discipline of waiting for Allah's forgiveness. For fifty days no one spoke to them. Finally, Allah revealed a verse to the Prophet ﷺ which declared that these three men were forgiven:

> *In the Name of Allah, the Beneficent, the Merciful*
>
> *Allah hath turned in mercy to the Prophet, and to the Muhājirīn and the Anṣār who followed him in the hour of hardship. After the hearts of a party of them had almost swerved aside, then He turned unto them in mercy. Lo! He is full of Pity, Merciful.*
>
> *And to the three also (did He turn in mercy) who were left behind, when the earth, vast as it is, was straitened for them, and their own souls were straitened for them till they understood that there is no refuge from Allah save toward Him. Then He turned unto them in mercy that they (too) might turn (repentant unto Him). Lo! Allah! He is the Relenting, the Merciful.*
>
> *O you who believe! Be careful of your duty to Allah, and be with the truthful.*

(*Koran* ix.117–119)

THE FAREWELL PILGRIMAGE

THE Prophet ﷺ had become the most powerful leader in the whole of Arabia. After the idols in the Ka'bah had been smashed and Quraysh had become Muslim, most of the other tribes of Arabia came to declare their Islam. The year in which they came was later to be called the Year of Deputations. As each tribe joined Islam, the Prophet Muḥammad ﷺ sent his men to teach them about their new religion.

Many people also came to Medina to question the Prophet ﷺ himself. One tribe sent a man called Dimām, who was large and strong. On arriving in Medina, he went straight to the mosque, where the Messenger of Allah ﷺ was sitting with some of his companions, and stood over the Prophet ﷺ. In a loud, rough voice he asked, 'Which of you is the son of 'Abd al-Muṭṭalib?' When the Prophet ﷺ answered him Dimām went on, 'I am going to ask you a hard question, so do not misunderstand me. I ask you to swear by Allah, your Allah, the Allah of those before you and the Allah of those who will come after you, has He sent you to us as a messenger?'

'Yes, He has', replied the Prophet ﷺ.

'Has Allah instructed you to order us to serve Him; to pray these five prayers; to pay alms; to fast; to make the pilgrimage and to follow the other laws of Islam?' continued Dimām.

When the Prophet ﷺ answered that Allah had indeed instructed him in this way, Dimām became a Muslim and, as he left, added, 'Then I will do the things we are told to do and avoid the things we are forbidden—no more and no less.'

As Dimām mounted his camel to leave, the Prophet ﷺ told the people around him, 'If this man is sincere, he will go to Paradise.' When Dimām reached his people they all thought he had gone mad but by nightfall, after he had finished speaking, there was not one among them that had not accepted Islam.

When the time came for the yearly pilgrimage, it was proclaimed that the Prophet ﷺ would be going to Mecca. The Muslims flocked to Medina from all over Arabia to join him on his journey to the Ka'bah. As the tribes arrived they camped around the city until they finally numbered more than thirty thousand. The Prophet ﷺ went out with his family and friends to meet them and to lead them on the pilgrimage, but before setting off, he led all the Muslims in prayer. After the prayers, the Prophet ﷺ got on his camel and headed towards Mecca followed by the pilgrims, all of whom, for the first time in centuries, worshipped Allah, the One God.

The Prophet ﷺ and his companions were deeply moved by the sight of the huge number of Muslims accompanying them to Mecca, carrying no arms, and fearing no one. They could not help but remember their original flight from Mecca when they had been so few in number and were forced to leave in order to avoid the anger of Quraysh.

Throughout the journey the Muslims repeated a prayer taught to them by the Prophet ﷺ, which he in turn had received from the Archangel Gabriel. This prayer, the *talbiyah*, has been part of the Hajj ritual ever since. It is in answer to the call Abraham was commanded to make when he and Ishmael finished building the Ka'bah.

> Labaik alahumma labaik, labaik la sharika laka labaik
> in al-hamd wa al-ni'amatu laka wal-mulk, la sharika laka.
>
> Here I am, O Allah, at Thy service. Here I am,
> Thou art without partner, here I am. All Praise and blessings
> are thine, and Dominion! Thou art without partner!

After ten days the pilgrims marched at sunset through the same pass by which they had entered on the Day of Conquest of Mecca. When they reached the Ka'bah, the Prophet ﷺ stood before it in prayer, then he and all the Muslims walked around it seven times saying their prayer aloud. Next, just as Abraham had done, they went towards the Mount of Mercy at 'Arafah, which the Prophet ﷺ ascended on a camel.

From the mountain he led the people in prayer and then spoke to them as they stood assembled on the vast plain below. What the Prophet ﷺ said is known as the 'Farewell Sermon', because it was the last speech the Prophet ﷺ made before he died. He said, 'Surely you will meet your Lord and He will question you about your works.' He asked the Muslims to take their guidance from the Koran and from his own example. This, he said, was the best way to live. He ordered them to cease living in the way they had before Islam. Revenge, one of the oldest traditions in Arabia, was ended forever; usury was prohibited; property was to be respected. Things which previously were forbidden during the four sacred months of the year were now forbidden at all times. He then commanded, 'Know that every Muslim is a Muslim's brother', which was a completely new idea to the tribes who had so often quarrelled in the past. He also said, 'Allah has given everyone his due—exactly what each one deserves.' After each point the Prophet ﷺ asked, 'Have I explained it well? Is it perfectly clear?'

Everyone answered, 'Yes.' For these were the people who would have to pass on the Prophet's message and instructions to those who were unable to be present that day and to future generations.

The Prophet ﷺ said, 'I have left you two things. If you hold on to them you will be saved. They are Allah's Book and the words of your Prophet.' He then asked, 'Have I not conveyed the message?'

The multitude shouted out, 'By Allah, yes!'

The Prophet ﷺ ended, 'O Allah! Bear witness to that.'

In the Name of Allah, the Beneficent, the Merciful

. . . This day those who disbelieve are in despair of
(ever harming) your religion; so do not fear them, but fear Me!
This day I have perfected your religion for you,
and I have completed My favour unto you, and
have chosen for you as a religion AL-ISLAM . . .

(*Koran* v.3)

Many Muslims started to shed tears, knowing that if the Prophet ﷺ had completed his message, his life must be near its end.

After spending the rest of the 'Day of 'Arafah' in prayer and contemplation, the Muslims began to complete the pilgrimage by returning to Mecca with the *talbiyah* prayer still on their lips. The first night of the return journey was spent at Muzdalifah. Here they gathered pebbles, which they carried with them the next day to Mina. There they stood before a huge rock and stoned it in remembrance of Abraham's meeting with the Devil in that very place. When Abraham received the order from Allah to sacrifice his son Ishmael as a test of his faith, the Devil had tried to convince him not to do it. He came to Abraham at Mina, as he was on his way to carry out Allah's command, but Abraham took some stones and hurled them at the Devil to drive him away. Since the casting of stones at Mina on the Prophet's 'Farewell Pilgrimage', this has become another ritual which Muslims perform on the annual pilgrimage to remind them that they, too, must continue to drive the Devil away when he tries to prevent them from being obedient to Allah.

After throwing the stones, the pilgrims sacrificed sheep and camels and gave the meat to the poor. In this way the great faith of Abraham was remembered, for when he had been ready to sacrifice Ishmael, Allah had sent a sheep in his place. The Muslims then completed the pilgrimage by again circling the Ka'bah seven times. They then cut their hair and nails and changed out of their white clothes to show they had returned to their daily lives. Before returning to Medina, the Muslims spent three nights in the valley at Mina, where the final preparations were made for the journey home.

As for the Prophet ﷺ, he made one final visit before leaving Mecca. This was to the grave of his devoted wife, Khadījah, who had been the first person to believe in Allah's Revelation through him. The Prophet ﷺ knew that this would be the last time he would see the grave, or Mecca, because during the pilgrimage he had received the chapter of the Koran called 'Help', from which he knew that his death was not far away.

In the Name of Allah, the Beneficent, the Merciful

When Allah's help and triumph comes
And thou seest mankind entering the religion of Allah in troops,
Then hymn the praises of thy Lord, and seek forgiveness of
Him. Lo! He is ever ready to show mercy.

(*Koran* cx.1–3)

THE PROPHET'S DEATH

ONE NIGHT, shortly after his return to Medina, the Prophet ﷺ woke up at midnight and asked his servant 'Abd Allāh to saddle his mule. They then left the house and went to the Baqī al-Gharqad, the burial ground of the Muslims. There the Prophet ﷺ stood in front of the graves and, as though he could see the Muslims buried in them, spoke to them and prayed over them. Later, 'Abd Allāh reported, 'The Prophet ﷺ told me that he was ordered to pray for the dead and that I was to go with him.'

After the Prophet ﷺ had prayed he turned to 'Abd Allāh and said, 'I can choose between all the riches of this world, a long life, and then Paradise, or meeting my Lord and entering Paradise now.' 'Abd Allāh begged him to choose a long, rich life, followed by Paradise, but the Prophet ﷺ told him that he had already chosen to meet his Lord now rather than remain in the world.

The following morning the Prophet ﷺ awoke with a terrible headache, but despite this he led the prayers at the mosque. From what he said afterwards to the people assembled there, they understood that his death was near. The Prophet ﷺ praised his best friend, Abū Bakr, who had begun to weep, and told everyone that he knew they would all meet again at a pool in Paradise. He added, however, that although he was sure they would always worship Allah alone, he feared that the pleasures of the world would attract them, and they would begin to compete with one another for material possessions, forgetting spiritual things.

Soon after, the Prophet ﷺ requested that he be moved to the room of 'Ā'ishah, one of his wives. As the days passed his fever grew worse, until one day he was so ill that he could not even get to the mosque, which was next to where 'Ā'ishah lived. The Prophet ﷺ told 'Ā'ishah to tell the Muslims to let

Abū Bakr, her father, lead the prayer, which made them very sad for this was the first time anyone had taken the Prophet's place.

Later, on the 12th day of Rabi al-Awal, in the 11th year of Islam (June 8th 632 A.D.), the Prophet ﷺ heard the voices of the people in prayer. With great effort he got up and looked from his door at all the Muslims who were assembled in rows behind Abū Bakr; he smiled with great satisfaction. Abū Bakr saw him and stepped back to give the Prophet ﷺ his place. The Muslims were happy, thinking he was going to pray with them as before, but the Prophet Muḥammad ﷺ, who looked radiantly beautiful that day, signalled to them to continue on their own. He prayed in a sitting position at the right of Abū Bakr, after which he went back inside and lay his head on 'Ā'ishah's lap. He was in such pain that his daughter Fāṭimah cried out in pity. Then the Prophet ﷺ said, 'There is no pain for your father after this day; truly, death has appeared to me. We must all suffer it till the Day of Judgement.' As he lay there, 'Ā'ishah remembered that he had once said, 'Allah never takes a Prophet to Himself without giving him the choice.' Then she heard the Prophet ﷺ speak. His last words were, 'Nay, rather the Exalted Communion of Paradise.'

'Ā'ishah then said to herself, 'So, by Allah, he is not choosing us!'

When the people in the mosque heard that the Prophet ﷺ was dead, they were filled with grief. 'Umar could not, and would not, believe it, and exclaimed that it was not true. Abū Bakr then went out and spoke gently to the people, saying 'All praise belongs to Allah! O people, whoever worshipped Muḥammad, Muḥammad is dead. But for him who worships Allah, Allah is living and never dies.' He then recited this verse from the Koran which had been revealed after the battle of Uhud:

In the Name of Allah, the Beneficent, the Merciful

Muḥammad is but a messenger, messengers (the like of whom)
have passed away before him. Will it be that, when he dies or is slain,
you will turn back on your heels? He who turns back
does no hurt to Allah, and Allah will reward
the thankful.

No soul can ever die except by Allah's permission and at a term appointed. Whoso desires the reward of the world, We bestow on him thereof; and whosoever desires the reward of the Hereafter, We bestow on him thereof. We shall reward the thankful.

(*Koran* iii.144–45)

After this the people pledged their loyalty to Abū Bakr, whom the Prophet ﷺ had chosen to lead the prayer. Abū Bakr accepted and concluded what he had to say with these words:

> 'Obey me so long as I obey Allah and His Messenger. But if I disobey Allah and His Messenger, you owe me no obedience. Arise for your prayer, Allah have mercy upon you!'

The people rose and asked him: 'Where will the Prophet ﷺ be buried?' Abū Bakr remembered that the Prophet ﷺ had said, 'No Prophet dies who is not buried on the spot where he died.' And so the Prophet ﷺ was buried in a grave dug in the floor of 'Ā'ishah's room, in the house next to the mosque. The spot became known as the Haram al-Nabawi and Muslims from all over the world go there to pray and to give their blessings and greetings of peace to the Prophet Muḥammad ﷺ.

And Lo! thine verily will be a reward unfailing.
And Lo! thou art of a tremendous nature.

(*Koran* lxviii.3–4)

A COLLECTION OF HADITH FROM AL-SHAMA'IL BY AL-TIRMIDHI

On the face and features of the Prophet ﷺ

Anas ibn Mālik says that the Prophet of Allah ﷺ had a moderate stature, being neither very tall nor very short. His person was finely symmetrical and the hair of his head was neither very curly nor very straight; his complexion was tawny.

Ibrāhīm ibn Muḥammad ibn ʿAlī ibn Abī Ṭālib says. . . . His heart was much more liberal than that of any other person; in speech he was more truthful than all other men; by nature he was gentler than all, in social life nobler than everyone. Whoever happened to see him suddenly was struck with awe; and whoever came to know him by association could not help loving him. The narrator says that he has never known the like of him before or after.

Hind says that the Prophet ﷺ was grand, in fact he was grandeur itself. His face shone like the full moon. He was of middle height, inclined to tallness but was shorter than very tall people. . . . He walked softly and firmly with a rapid pace and a slightly forward bend, as if he were descending from a higher to a lower level. Whenever he looked at anything he would look straight into it; his eyes were always downcast, directed more towards the earth than towards the sky. The Prophet ﷺ would often look at the things of the world from the corners of his eyes. He would make his disciples walk before him, and would make his salutations first, when he met another Muslim.

Jābir ibn Samurah says, 'The Prophet of Allah ﷺ had a wide mouth. The eyes were of light brown hue and the heels had little flesh. I saw the Prophet ﷺ on a moonlit night. He had a red cloak over his body and I looked attentively in turn towards him and the moon. He certainly appeared to me to be more beautiful than the moon itself.'

Abū Hurayrah says that the Prophet ﷺ had a white complexion as if he were made of silver. There was a moderate wave in his hair.

Sa'īd al-Jurayrī relates that he heard Abū Tufayl saying that he had seen the Prophet of Allah; . . . Then Sa'īd asked him to give a description of the Prophet ﷺ. He replied that the Prophet ﷺ was reddish-white in hue, beautiful and of moderate temper.

Abū Bakr said to the Prophet ﷺ that although he was in good condition physically, it was strange that he appeared old. He ﷺ replied that the verses[1] mentioned below had made him old, because in those verses are descriptions of the Day of Resurrection and of hell. Anxiety and sorrow for mankind had made him old.

Abū Sa'īd al-Khudri says that when the Prophet of Allah wore new apparel he would say that all praise was due to Allah who had given him that garment, and he would then pray for the sanctity of the clothes . . . Samurah ibn Jundub relates that the Prophet ﷺ said; 'Wear white clothes; verily they are very pure and clean; and shroud your dead in it.'

Abū Hurayrah narrates that the Prophet ﷺ said, 'When any one amongst you puts on shoes, he ought to begin with the right foot. When he removes his shoes, he should start with the left one so that the right one is last.'

'Ā'ishah says that in all personal habits, such as combing the hair, wearing shoes and performing ablutions, the Prophet ﷺ preferred to begin from the right.

Abū Hurayrah says that he did not see anything more beautiful than the Prophet ﷺ from whose face the sun seemed to shine, and he did not see anybody quicker in his walk than the Prophet ﷺ for the ground seemed to roll itself up for him. His disciples used to exert themselves in keeping up with him when the Prophet ﷺ walked leisurely. Ibrāhīm ibn Muḥammad, who was one of the descendants of 'Alī ibn Abī Ṭālib, says that when 'Alī described the Prophet ﷺ he used to say that the Prophet ﷺ walked with vigour as if he were descending to a low level.

'Abdur Rahmān, son of Abū Bakr, narrates on the authority of his father, that the Prophet ﷺ asked whether he should not inform them about the greatest of sins. . . . Then the Prophet ﷺ said that they were setting up rivals to God and disobedience to parents. . . . The Prophet ﷺ said in continuation that lying was to be considered among the greater sins.

[1] The verses of *Hud* (chapter 11 of the Koran), *al-Waqi'a* (chapter 56), *al-Mursalat* (Chapter 77), *'Amma Yatasa'lun* (chapter 78), and *Idha'sh-Shamsu Kuwwirat* (chapter 81).

Abū Ayyūb al-Anṣāri says that they were in the company of the Prophet ﷺ one day and food was placed before him. There was great blessing in the food of which they partook first but less blessing in the food which they ate last. Then he said, 'O Prophet ﷺ! How did this happen?' The Prophet ﷺ replied that they had mentioned the name of Allah when they began to eat, but when later on a person sat down and began to eat without repeating the name of Allah, Satan ate with him.

'Ā'ishah narrates that the Prophet ﷺ said that in case a person forgets to say 'Bismillah' (In the Name of Allah) when beginning to eat, it would do if he repeated the name of God, when he remembers, in this way: 'Let it be in the name of God at its beginning and at its end.' 'Umar ibn Abī Salmah says that he went to the Prophet ﷺ. Then the Prophet ﷺ said, 'Come near, O child! Mention the name of God and eat with the right hand and eat from the side that is near you.' Abū Sa'īd al-Khudrī says that the Prophet ﷺ, when he finished eating, used to say, 'All praise is due to God who has fed us and given us drink and made us Muslims.'

Anas ibn Mālik says, 'Verily Allah is pleased with those who eat a morsel or drink a sip and praise Him for it.'

It was related that the Prophet ﷺ said, 'If any one of you is given a fragrant flower he should not refuse it because flowers come from paradise.'

'Ā'ishah says that the Prophet ﷺ did not speak fast like other people but distinctly, pronouncing every word separately so that the person who sat near him could remember his words.

Hind bint Abī Hālah . . . said that the Prophet ﷺ generally remained silent. He did not speak unnecessarily. He used to begin and finish his talk clearly. He spoke in order to enjoin righteousness or to forbid wrongdoing. It was not idle talk and he spoke eloquently. He was never unjust towards any person, nor did he allow any person to be looked down upon. . . . The world and the things in it could not annoy him. But when truth was disregarded then nothing could pacify his anger unless and until religious injunctions were enforced. He did not take offence at any remark of a personal nature, neither did he revenge himself upon anybody. . . . He looked away whenever he became angry and looked down when he was pleased. Most of his laughter was smiling.

Abū Hurayrah narrates that the Prophet ﷺ said that the best words which the Arab poets had chanted were the lines of Labīd, beginning: 'Beware! Everything except Allah is perishable.'

Al-Barā' ibn 'Āzib narrates that when the Prophet ﷺ lay down on his bed he used to put his right palm below his right cheek and used to say 'O Allah! save me from the punishment on the day when Thou wilt raise Thy creatures.'

When the Prophet ﷺ went to bed he said: 'O Allah! In Thy name I lie down and in Thy Name I arise'; and when he awoke he said: 'All praise to Allah who has revived us after we were made to die and unto Him shall be the Resurrection.'

'Ā'ishah says that when the Prophet ﷺ went to bed every night he would join his palms and blow upon them and read the following *surāhs* of the Koran, namely: *Qulhuwa'llahu Ahad*, *Qul A'udhu bi Rabbi'l-Falaq* and *Qul A'udhu bi Rabbi'n-Nas*. And then he would pass his hands over his body as far as he could. He would begin by rubbing his head and face and the front portion of his body.

The voluntary fasting of the Prophet ﷺ

Anas ibn Mālik was asked regarding the fasting of the Prophet ﷺ. He replied that the Prophet ﷺ in certain months kept fasting so long that they thought he would not break the fast at all and in certain other months he broke the fast for such a long time that they thought he would not keep the fast any more. 'If you wanted to see the Prophet ﷺ offering prayers at night you would see him doing so and if you wanted to see him sleeping then you would find him doing that also.'

'Ā'ishah says that the Prophet ﷺ fasted on Mondays and Thursdays. 'Ā'ishah says further that the Prophet observed fasting for a larger number of days in Sha'ban than in any other month.

The Prophet ﷺ liked only those deeds which the performer observed constantly. Abū Salih says that he asked 'Ā'ishah and Umm Salamah what acts were liked very much by the Prophet ﷺ. Both replied: Such acts as can always be performed regularly, whether great or small.

On the Prophet's way of reading the Koran

Someone asked Umm Salamah concerning the Prophet's way of reading the Koran. She said that the reading of the Koran by the Prophet ﷺ was clear and every letter was pronounced distinctly.

Ibn 'Abbās says that the reading of the Prophet ﷺ was such that when he read in his room a man in the courtyard could hear him distinctly.

On the humility of the Prophet ﷺ

Anas ibn Mālik narrates that the Prophet ﷺ used to visit sick persons and attend funerals, ride on donkeys and accept even the invitations of slaves.

Ḥusayn says that . . . his father said that when the Prophet ﷺ came into the house, he divided his stay in the house into three parts. He kept one part for Allah, the Almighty, another for his family and the remaining part for himself. He divided his own part between himself and the people.

And he further said: 'Bring to me the needs of those persons who are not able to bring them to me, for the feet of that person who conveys the needs of persons who are unable to come to a leader themselves will be firm on the day of Resurrection.'

Ḥusayn said . . . his father replied that the Prophet ﷺ invoked the name of Allah at the time of sitting down and of standing up.

On the behaviour of the Prophet ﷺ

Anas ibn Mālik says . . . for anything that he did the Prophet never asked, 'Why did you do that?' nor did the Prophet ﷺ take anyone to task for any fault of omission by saying, 'Why didn't you do it?' The Prophet ﷺ was the best of mankind as regards manners.

'Ā'ishah says . . . nor did he return evil for evil, but he used to forgive and pardon. 'Ā'ishah says that the Prophet ﷺ never struck anybody except in *jihad* (holy war).

Anas ibn Mālik says that the Prophet ﷺ did not keep anything for himself for the coming day.

On seeing the Prophet ﷺ *in a dream*

'Abd Allāh ibn Mas'ūd says that the Prophet ﷺ had said, 'Whoever sees me in a dream truly sees me because Satan cannot assume my shape.'

THE PROPHET'S FAMILY

The Prophet's Wives

The Prophet's first wife was Khadījah, the daughter of Khuwaylid. She was a tradeswoman of honour and great wealth, twice widowed before her marriage to the Prophet ﷺ. He was twenty-five and she was forty at that time. She was his only wife for nearly twenty-five years, and the mother of his children: Zaynab, Ruqayyah, Umm Kulthūm, and Fāṭimah. Also there were two sons, al-Qāsim and ʿAbd Allāh, who both died as infants.

After the death of Khadījah, the Prophet ﷺ married Sawdah from the tribe of Banu ʿĀmir. Her father was one of the earliest converts to Islam. She was the widow of one of the Muslim companions who emigrated to Abyssinia but died upon his return to Mecca.

At this time he was engaged to ʿĀ'ishah, the daughter of Abū Bakr-as-Siddīq, the Companion of the Prophet ﷺ. Since ʿĀ'ishah was still too young to marry, the marriage was postponed for three more years. It is from ʿĀ'ishah that many of the Hadith have come.

Later the Prophet ﷺ married other women. One of them was Ḥafṣah, the daughter of ʿUmar ibn al-Khattāb. She became a widow when her husband died as a result of wounds received in the battle of Badr. She was very young when she was widowed. The Prophet ﷺ was married to her after the second or third year of the *Ḥijrah*.

Another widow whom the Prophet ﷺ married was Zaynab, the daughter of Khuzaymah. Her husband died a martyr in the battle of Badr. She was known as the mother of the poor' because of her generosity and special kindness to the poor.

Umm Salamah was the daughter of Abū Umayyah ibn al-Mughīrah one of the leaders of Quraysh. She was first married to Abū Salamah and migrated with him to Abyssinia. When he later died of his wounds from the battle of Uhud, she became one of the Prophet's wives.

A year after the battle of the Trench, the Prophet ﷺ fought another battle with Banu al-Mustaliq and defeated them. Barrah came with a lot of booty to the Muslim camp, being the daughter of the Chief of her people. The Prophet ﷺ, who saved her from humiliation and married her, changed her name to Juwayriyah.

Zaynab bint Jaḥsh was the daughter of a sister of the Prophet's father ʿAbd Allāh. The Prophet ﷺ gave her in marriage to his adopted son Zayd ibn Hārithah who was a freed slave. He divorced her later in the fifth year of the *ḥijrah*. Islam does not recognise adoption, and a verse from the *Koran* was revealed to the Prophet ﷺ ordering him to marry Zaynab.

Umm Habībah, the daughter of Abū Sufyān, embraced Islam and together with her first husband migrated to Abyssinia, where he converted to Christianity. As a result, this marriage with Umm Habībah was disrupted. Later on, her husband died. The Prophet ﷺ was informed of her difficulties and arranged, through the Negus, to marry her. To this she consented.

Ṣafiyyah was the daughter of the chief of the Jewish tribe of Banu Nadir. Her father was one of the Prophet's bitterest enemies. When this tribe was expelled from Medina, her father settled in Khaybar. After the fall of Khaybar in the seventh year of the Hijrah, Ṣafiyyah was captured. She converted to Islam and the Prophet ﷺ married her.

Maymūnah was the daughter of Hārith of the Ḣawāzin tribe and a sister in law of Al-ʿAbbās, the Prophet's uncle. She lived as a widow in Mecca. The Prophet ﷺ married her when he and his followers entered Mecca after the years of exile.

After the treaty of Hudaybiyah, the Prophet ﷺ sent personal invitations to Syria, Egypt and other countries to join Islam. Māriya, a Copt maiden, was sent as a gift to the Prophet ﷺ by Muqawqis, the chief of the Copts in Egypt. She was the only one after Khadījah to bear the Prophet ﷺ a child, a son called Ibrāhīm, who died in childhood.

The Prophet's Daughters

Zaynab married Abū al 'As Ibn-Rabi', whose mother was Khadījah's sister. Ruqayyah and Umm Kulthūm married ʿUtbah and Utaybah, the sons of Abū Lahab. These marriages, however, broke up at the coming of Islam. Later Uthmān Ibn ʿAffān married Ruqayyah and after her death, her sister Umm Kulthūm.

Fāṭimah married ʿAli ibn Abū Ṭālib, the Prophet's cousin, and gave birth to Hasan, Ḥusayn and Zaynab.

GLOSSARY

'ABD ALLĀH: 'Abd al-Muṭṭalib's youngest son. Father of the Prophet ﷺ.

'ABD ALLĀH IBN UBAYY: One of the rulers of Yathrib before the *Ḥijrah*. He became a Muslim but secretly plotted with the Meccans against the Prophet ﷺ.

'ABD AL-MUṬṬALIB: Son of Hashim. He took the place of his father as the head of Quraysh. He dug the well of Zamzam.

'ABD ALLĀH IBN ABŪ RABI'AH: Was sent with 'Amr ibn al-'Āṣ to Abyssinia.

'ABDU MANĀF: Son of Quṣayy; took over as leader of the Quraysh after his father's death.

ABRAHAH: King of Yemen who came to Mecca with a big army to destroy the Ka'bah.

ABRAHAM (*IBRĀHĪM*): The founding father of the three monotheistic (worshipping one God only) religions—Judaism, Christianity and Islam. The descendants of his son Ishmael (*Ismā'īl*) formed the tribe of Quraysh, which is the tribe of the Prophet Muḥammad ﷺ.

ABŪ BAKR: A rich and much respected merchant of Mecca. The first man to believe in the Prophet ﷺ and embrace Islam. He was the Prophet's closest friend and companion.

ABŪ DUJĀNAH: One of the great *Ānṣar* warriors. It was he who died shielding the Prophet ﷺ with his own body during the battle of Uhud.

ABŪ JAHL: One of the important men of Quraysh. Violently opposed to Islam, he did many things to harm the Prophet ﷺ. He was killed at Badr.

ABŪ LAHAB: One of the Prophet Muḥammad's uncles, who was a great enemy of Islam. He is referred to in the *Koran* in *sūrah* cxi.

ABŪ SUFYĀN: One of the leaders of Quraysh who led the unbelievers in their fight against the Prophet ﷺ. He finally became a Muslim. His wife was Hind.

ABŪ ṬĀLIB: The Prophet's uncle, father of 'Alī, one of the respected men of Quraysh. He took care of the Prophet ﷺ after his grandfather died and continued to protect him until his own death.

'ADDĀS: A Christian servant of one of the big tribes of Tā'if and the only person from this town to believe in the Prophet ﷺ at the time of his first visit there.

ADHĀN: Call to prayer.

'A'ISHAH: The Prophet's wife and daughter of Abū Bakr.

AL-'ABBĀS: One of the uncles of the Prophet ﷺ. Converted to Islam and joined the Muslims just as they were about to enter Mecca.

'ALĪ: Son of Abū Ṭālib. First cousin of the Prophet ﷺ. 'Alī later married Fāṭimah, the youngest daughter of the Prophet ﷺ.

ALLĀHU AKBAR: Phrase meaning 'God alone is Great'.
ALMS: Money, clothes or food given to the poor.
ĀMINAH: Āminah bint Wahb. The mother of the Prophet ﷺ.
'AMR IBN AL-'ĀṢ: An important and clever man from Quraysh; was sent to Abyssinia to bring back the first Muslim emigrants. Later became one of the great warriors of Islam.
ANṢĀR: The inhabitants of Medina who became Muslims and asked the Prophet ﷺ to come and live with them.
APOSTLE: Person sent to teach men about God.
ASSALAMU ALEIKUM WA RAHMATULLAH WA BARAKATUHU: Phrase used by the Muslims in greeting, meaning: 'May the Peace, Mercy and Grace of Allah be upon you.'
BAḤĪRÀ: A monk who lived in the desert on the Quraysh caravan route to Syria.
BANI HĀSHIM: The branch of Quraysh to which the Prophet ﷺ belonged.
BANI QURAYẒAH: A Jewish tribe who were living in Yathrib at the time the Prophet ﷺ arrived there. Several times they betrayed their covenant with the Prophet ﷺ, forcing him to fight them.
BEDOUIN: Nomadic Arabs of the desert, usually shepherds.
BILĀL: The Slave of Umayyah ibn Khalaf. He became a Muslim against the will of his master and was persecuted cruelly but never lost his faith. Later he became the first *mu'adhdhin* (the person who calls the *adhān*).
BISMILLĀH: The phrase meaning 'In the Name of Allah the Merciful, the Compassionate'.
BOOTY: Things captured from an enemy in war.
BURĀQ: Animal ridden by the Prophet Muḥammad ﷺ on his ascent to heaven (the *Isra'* and *Mi'raj*).
CARAVAN: A group of travellers, usually merchants with their goods.
CLAN: Large family or tribe.
CONGREGATION: Gathering of people for prayer.
CONVERT: To change from one state into another, usually said of religion.
COPT: An Egyptian Christian.
DESCENDANTS: People originating from a certain person (children, grand-children, etc.).
DESTINED: Fated, already decided by God.
FAMINE: Scarcity of food.
FAST: To go without food and water, e.g. the month of Ramadan.
FIṬRAH: The pure original nature God gave to man.
GABRIEL (JIBRĪL): The Archangel who conveyed the Revelation of the *Koran* to the Prophet ﷺ from Allah.

GRAZE: To feed on grass, as sheep do.
GUARDIAN: One who is responsible for someone (e.g. a child), a place, or thing.
HADITH: An account of what the Prophet ﷺ said or did, or his silent approval of something said or done in his presence.
HAGAR (HAAJAR): Abraham's second wife and mother of his first son Ishmael.
ḤALĪMAH: A Bedouin woman from Bani Sa'd, who cared for the Prophet ﷺ during his early childhood.
ḤAMZAH: The Prophet's uncle; one of the bravest and strongest of the Muslims. Fought at Badr and was killed in Uhud.
HĀSHIM: Son of Abdu Manāf. Organized the caravan journeys of Quraysh to Syria and Yemen. As a result Mecca grew rich and became a large and important centre of trade.
HERACLIUS: Emperor of the Eastern Roman Empire.
HERMIT: A holy man who lives far away from people.
ḤIJRAH: The flight from Mecca to Medina; emigration.
HIND: Abū Sufyān's wife.
IMĀM: A man who leads the Muslims in prayer.
ISHMAEL (ISMĀ'ĪL): The first son of Abraham from his wife Hagar. Settled in Mecca where he helped his father rebuild the Ka'bah. From his descendants came Quraysh.
ISLAM: Religion revealed to the Prophet Muḥammad ﷺ.
JA'FAR IBN ABŪ ṬĀLIB: A cousin of the Prophet ﷺ and brother of 'Alī, he was the spokesman of the Muslims who emigrated to Abyssinia.
KHADĪJAH: The Prophet Muḥammad's first and only wife until her death. She was the first to believe in the Prophet ﷺ and to accept as true the Message he brought from Allah.
KHĀLID IBN AL-WALĪD: A great warrior, very skilled at warfare. He planned the defeat of the Muslims at Uhud, but later converted to Islam and fought even more strongly for his new faith.
MARTYR: One who dies in the cause of God.
MAYSARAH: Khadījah's slave. Accompanied the Prophet ﷺ on his journey with Khadījah's caravans.
MINARET: Tower from which the call to prayer is made.
MOSQUE: Building in which Muslims pray.
MUSLIM: One who submits to God, usually referring to the followers of the Prophet Muḥammad ﷺ.
OASIS: A small area in the desert where water and trees are to be found.
PARADISE: Place to which the souls of good people go after death.
PILGRIMAGE: Journey to a holy place, e.g. Hajj.

PROPHET: A man who comes with a message from God.
QURAYSH: The descendants of Ishmael, son of Abraham, who became the most important tribe in Mecca. The tribe of the Prophet ﷺ.
QUṢAYY: One of the leaders of Quraysh who became ruler over Mecca. He held the keys of the Ka'bah. (He is the great-great-great grandfather of the Prophet ﷺ.)
REPENT: To regret having done wrong and to vow not to repeat it.
REVELATION: Truth sent to man from God.
SACRIFICE: Making an offering to God; to give up a thing for some noble reason.
SA'D IBN MU'ĀDH: One of the *Anṣār* (the people of Yathrib). He fought beside the Prophet ﷺ at Badr and other battles. He died after the battle of the Trench.
SANCTUARY: A sacred place; a refuge.
SARAH: Abraham's first wife and mother of his second son Isaac.
SCHOLARS: Learned people.
SCRIPTURES: Holy book or writing.
SCROLL: A roll of paper or skin to be used for writing.
SEAL OF THE PROPHETS: The Prophet Muḥammad ﷺ who was the last Messenger from God to man.
SHEIKH: Head of a tribe; old, respected or learned man.
SIDRAT AL-MUNTAHA: The Lote-tree of the Uttermost, limit of the heavens.
SIEGE: To surround a town in order to capture it.
SLANDER: A lie that damages the reputation of a person.
SŪRAH: Chapter from the *Koran*.
TAWAF: Ritual encircling of the Ka'bah.
'UBAYDAH IBN AL-ḤĀRITH: One of the three Muslims picked by the Prophet ﷺ to start the fighting at the battle of Badr.
'UMAR IBN AL-KHAṬṬTAB: One of the bravest and most important men of Quraysh, who greatly influenced the course of Islam after his conversion to the faith.
UMAYYAH IBN KHALAF: One of the important men of Mecca and a great enemy of Islam. Fought at Badr and was killed by his former slave, Bilāl.
WADI: Shallow valley.
WAḤSHĪ: The Abyssinian slave who killed Ḥamzah.

This children's book on the life of the Prophet Muhammad ﷺ is taken from traditional Muslim biographical literature, including Hadith. Passages from the Koran are used throughout to reinforce the stories. The material is authentic and the style lively and attractive.

Although the book has been written for children of 10 to 15 years of age it can be usefully read by anyone as an introduction to the life of the Prophet ﷺ because of its completeness and clarity.

There are 32 colour illustrations and every care has been taken over authentic detail. There has been no attempt to portray either the Prophet ﷺ or his Companions. The illustrations are representative of traditional Islamic life as lived in any Arab country and portray scenes that have occurred in those countries for over 1000 years.

Leila Azzam

Mrs Azzam is the niece of the late Dr Abdul Wahab Azzam, who was rector of Cairo University, founder and first Rector of Riyadh University, and prominent Muslim writer. She is also the daughter-in-law of the late Dr Abdur Rahman Azzam, founder of the Arab League and author of the *Eternal Message of Muhammad*. Mrs Azzam was born in Cairo and is a graduate of the Faculty of Arts and Literature, Cairo University. She has lived with her husband, Dr Omar Azzam, in Saudi Arabia, Lebanon and France, and is now living in Cambridge, England, where her four children are receiving their education.

Aisha Gouverneur

Mrs Gouverneur was born Virginia Gray Henry in Kentucky, USA, and became a Muslim in 1968. She took a BA in comparative religion from Sarah Lawrence College, Bronxville, New York, and has an MA in Education from Michigan University. Mrs Gouverneur has also studied at Al-Azhar University, Cairo, and has taught for more than ten years. She lived in Egypt for over ten years and now lives with her husband and two children in Cambridge, England.